TRANSFORMATION IN EGYPTIAN JOURNALISM

RISJ CHALLENGES

CHALLENGES present findings, analysis and recommendations from Oxford's Reuters Institute for the Study of Journalism. The Institute is dedicated to the rigorous, international comparative study of journalism, in all its forms and on all continents. CHALLENGES muster evidence and research to take forward an important argument, beyond the mere expression of opinions. Each text is carefully reviewed by an editorial committee, drawing where necessary on the advice of leading experts in the relevant fields. CHALLENGES remain, however, the work of authors writing in their individual capacities, not a collective expression of views from the Institute.

EDITORIAL COMMITTEE

Timothy Garton Ash
Ian Hargreaves
David Levy
Geert Linnebank
John Lloyd
Rasmus Kleis Nielsen
James Painter
Robert Picard
Jean Seaton
Katrin Voltmer
David Watson

The editorial advisers on this CHALLENGE were David Gardner and David Levy

TRANSFORMATIONS IN EGYPTIAN JOURNALISM

NAOMI SAKR

Published by I.B.Tauris & Co. Ltd in association with
the Reuters Institute for the Study of Journalism, University of Oxford

Published in 2013 by I.B.Tauris & Co Ltd
6 Salem Road, London W2 4BU
175 Fifth Avenue, New York NY 10010
www.ibtauris.com

Distributed in the United States and Canada Exclusively by Palgrave Macmillan
175 Fifth Avenue, New York NY 10010

Copyright © 2013 Naomi Sakr

The right of Naomi Sakr to be identified as the author of this work has been asserted by the author in accordance with the Copyright, Designs and Patents Act 1988.

All rights reserved. Except for brief quotations in a review, this book, or any part thereof, may not be reproduced, stored in or introduced into a retrieval system, or transmitted, in any form or by any means, electronic, mechanical, photocopying, recording or otherwise, without the prior written permission of the publisher.

ISBN: 978 1 78076 589 1

A full CIP record for this book is available from the British Library
A full CIP record is available from the Library of Congress

Library of Congress Catalog Card Number: available

Typeset by 4word Ltd, Bristol
Printed and bound by CPI Group (UK) Ltd, Croydon, CR0 4YY

Contents

Executive Summary	vii
Note on Transliteration of Arabic	x
Historical Background to the Rise of Egyptian Journalism	xi
Guide to Egyptian Media Outlets Mentioned in the Report	xv
Names and Positions of Some Egyptian Journalists and Bloggers Mentioned in the Report	xvii

1.	**A National Rethink of News Values**	**1**
	Intensified repression of the media under SCAF	4
	A re-energised news sector	12
	Overview	19
2.	**Lessons from the Push for Professional Autonomy**	**21**
	Diverse approaches to the profession	23
	Individuals vs institutions	33
	Attitudes to social media as tools of news-gathering	41
3.	**Stimuli for a Public Service Ethos**	**49**
	Journalists' initiatives outside the state-run media	51
	Public ownership scenarios for state-run publications	56
	Support for an independent ERTU	63
	Implications for journalism in the private commercial sector	69
4.	**Nuts and Bolts of a New Deal**	**73**
	Unionisation in a legal limbo	76
	Voluntary codes at company level	81

	Scope for cross-border support	83
	Labour and NGO laws' impact on free speech	87
5.	**Conclusions**	**89**
	Recommendations	92

Notes   94

Bibliography   106

Acknowledgements   109

Executive Summary

Of the numerous transformations in Egyptian journalism throughout its long history, those that preceded and followed the revolutionary uprising of 25 January 2011 were especially momentous. In recent years, thanks to the rise of news leads and political information in expanding informal online spaces, journalists in mainstream media had the means to challenge misinformation from the dictatorial regime of Hosni Mubarak and his ruling National Democratic Party. Increasingly persistent popular protest, worsening corruption, and Egypt's first multi-candidate presidential election in 2005 emboldened them to do so. By September 2007, in the words of political blogger Baheyya at the time, a 'different breed' of journalists 'from starkly different schools' had come to the fore. With the turmoil of 2011–12 and an expanded search for a 'new kind of journalism' that would be credible, timely, relevant to ordinary people, and untainted by complicity with military rule or Mubarak's business cronies, the diversity multiplied.

Immediately after the handover of power to the Supreme Council of the Armed Forces (SCAF), headed by the man who was Mubarak's defence minister for 20 years, journalists were subject to two opposing trends. As Chapter 1 of this book illustrates, one trend was repressive, marked by retention of the old government-controlled press and broadcasting structures, the appointment of discredited figures to key media positions, military summons and prosecutions for coverage unfavourable to SCAF, and accusations that journalists were working to 'foreign agendas'. Most notably it was seen in violent physical attacks on reporters covering protests in Cairo and elsewhere. Elements of media repression continued even after Egypt's first civilian president, Mohammed Morsi, seemed to win a power struggle with the military in August 2012.

The other trend was potentially liberatory. Here it was a case of officials being called to account on prime-time television, ordinary citizens gaining access to papers seized from intelligence agencies, diverse groups collating information to counter military propaganda, and a proliferation of start-ups on a range of delivery platforms. Morsi's first decree, upon taking over legislative powers, did not end criminalisation of 'insults' to the president, but it did end pre-trial detention for journalists accused of such a crime.

As activist groups applied themselves to gathering and verifying footage of violence and human rights abuses by military and security forces, and media start-ups recruited protestors from Tahrir Square as trainees, definitions of journalistic professionalism came under scrutiny. Chapter 2 explores this process. For more than 50 years, laws and intimidation had obstructed professional behaviour and driven many journalists abroad, where they worked to diverse standards of autonomy and objectivity, depending on their employer. When high-profile, proven professionals started to return to Egypt and its changing media ecology after 2005, they helped to intensify the shake-up of local norms. Trials of strength with media owners came to a head in 2010. They continued into 2011–12 under SCAF and under Morsi, with established owners keeping the upper hand and public-spirited journalists facing more or less permanent job insecurity as a result. Traditionally under-represented in media professions, Morsi's Muslim Brotherhood supporters looked unversed in handling a free press. Meanwhile, the value of citizen journalism was such that mainstream media outlets tapped into blogs and social media resources on a regular and, in some cases, institutionalised basis. While examples of good practice in cross-media participatory reporting were welcomed, some professionals worried that Egyptian journalism had reached this phase without having first reached a consensus on norms of balance and fairness to all sides of a story.

However, one achievement of the 2011 uprising was to demonstrate how large a proportion of Egyptian public opinion will no longer tolerate having the public interest defined by a ruling elite. Young people, demographically important but sidelined economically, had by then already circumvented licensing restrictions through online radio and news services using Facebook and YouTube. Chapter 3 recounts how journalists in the shifting and uncertain post-Mubarak environment looked for ownership models and funding sources compatible with bringing content 'from the people to the people'. Demands for public ownership and a public service mandate were directed at the state-run print media, governed through the Higher Press Council by the upper house of Parliament, and the state broadcaster, attached to the Ministry of Information. Journalists

EXECUTIVE SUMMARY

pushing for change redoubled their efforts in late 2011 after state TV misreported a Coptic demonstration so badly it triggered a rebuke from the European Broadcasting Union. Yet under provisions of the old constitution retained by the March 2011 referendum, the majority political party of the day – in 2012 the Muslim Brothers' Freedom and Justice Party (FJP) – was authorised to keep the media in its grip. When a new constitution, drafted by an Islamist-dominated Constituent Assembly, was adopted by referendum in December 2012, it failed to inspire confidence that basic media freedoms would be guaranteed.

The ruling party's grip on the media encompassed the mechanisms by which journalists could legally represent their interests. Chapter 4 analyses how rules for representation affect the likelihood of reaching consensus on professional ethics. A general groundswell of union activity, under way before Mubarak fell, surfaced among journalists afterwards in the form of new unions or syndicates. These risked being denied recognition pending parliamentary approval for full trade union pluralism in workplaces as well as trades and professions. Civil society groups working towards journalism development were also left waiting, after the dissolution of Parliament in June 2012, for liberalisation of laws constraining their freedom of association, including association with international partners. International initiatives springing up in 2011 sought to incorporate Egyptian media managers, editors, and journalists in campaigns to promote transparency and accountability at a corporate level. But fear of further harassment by state prosecutors underlined the message of those calling on international donors to provide legal aid and enduring moral support.

The web of influences on Egyptian journalism gives rise to certain recommendations, set out in the report's final section, many of which have been stated by Egyptian and non-Egyptian bodies referenced in this book. The following list offers a summary of broad measures that would enable positive transformations described in these pages to proceed:

- Egypt's new constitution should feed into media law reform to end control over journalism by the executive branch of government, ruling party, state intelligence, and security forces.
- Media law reform should end criminal sanctions for journalists and bloggers whose work subjects the actions and policies of public figures and officials to critical scrutiny.
- The huge media operations currently under government control should be split into coherent, manageable, independent units run

- by journalists who command public respect. Core production units should be put into public ownership with a public service mandate.
- Regional journalism should be promoted through decentralisation of regional channels spun off from the state broadcaster and sustainable development of local radio and press.
- Trade union pluralism should be encouraged in accordance with Egypt's existing international commitments, so that journalists can choose how to be represented professionally and newly formed journalism unions have the option to federate.
- Journalists' inability to work professionally in a corrupt environment should be openly acknowledged through drafting of cross-platform standards for corporate governance and reporting based on ethics, transparency, and accountability.
- International bodies of broadcasters, media regulators, newspaper ombudsmen, and senior editors should encourage active Egyptian membership and be outspoken about membership obligations of fair and honest coverage.
- International donors should think creatively about the capacity-building needs of small-scale and/or regional news-gathering and distribution initiatives that cannot be self-sustaining until Egypt's creaking advertising industry catches up with journalistic innovation.

Note on Transliteration of Arabic

This book's simplified and often inconsistent method of transliterating Arabic uses 'k' for the letter *qaf* and sometimes 'aa' instead of an apostrophe to represent the letter *ain*.

Historical Background to the Rise of Egyptian Journalism

1821–2: Egypt's ruler, Mohammed Ali, orders printing of *Journal al-Khidiw* (Journal of the Khedive) in Arabic on local presses.

1876: First issue of *Al-Ahram* newspaper appears.

1882: British forces bombard Alexandria and take control of Egypt, putting down a revolt against the Ottoman ruler and European influence led by an army officer named Ahmad 'Urabi.

1896: First film screenings in Egypt take place in Alexandria and Cairo.

1906: Seven villagers in Denshway are ordered to be hanged and others flogged after they turn on British soldiers who accidentally injure an Egyptian woman while out pigeon-shooting.

1907–8: A number of nationalist and anti-occupation political parties form around newspapers such as *Al-Liwa*, *Al-Jarida*, and *Al-Mu'ayyad*.

1914: Egypt is declared a British Protectorate and placed under martial law, which includes press censorship.

1919: A delegation (*wafd*) of nationalist activists applies to the British High Commissioner for independence. The independence movement is violently suppressed and its leader, Saad Zaghloul, arrested and exiled, leading to prolonged unrest.

1923: Egypt gets a new constitution, with a parliamentary system, after Britain recognises a conditional form of independence. Elections in 1924 give Zaghloul's Wafd Party an overwhelming majority.

1928: Hassan al-Banna, son of a local imam, founds the Muslim Brotherhood.

1944: Mustafa and Ali Amin found weekly *Akhbar al-Youm*.

1947: Egyptians take over the country's radio network after cancelling the contract held by Marconi of the UK since radio was legalised in 1934.

1948: The state of Israel is created amid defeat of Egyptian and Arab armies.

1952–4: King Farouk abdicates in the face of the Free Officers' coup. Egypt is declared a republic, with Nasser taking over as president after the two-year presidency of Mohammed Naguib; all opposition parties are disbanded.

1953: Cairo Radio begins external broadcasting with Voice of the Arabs, reflecting Nasser's Arab nationalist ideology.

1956: Britain, France, and Israel invade after Nasser nationalises the Suez Canal; a ceasefire is achieved through interventions of the USA, USSR, and UN.

1960: First TV broadcast from Egyptian Radio and Television Union's Maspero building; Nasser nationalises the press.

1967: Voice of the Arabs misleads Egyptians into thinking their forces are winning the June Arab–Israeli war; Israeli forces capture Sinai and the Gaza Strip.

1973: Egyptian forces regain Sinai in the October War under Anwar Sadat, who succeeded Nasser on his death in 1970.

1978: Sadat forms the National Democratic Party in a limited move to revive political parties, which are then legally permitted to publish newspapers.

1979: Egyptian Radio and Television Union is granted legal monopoly over terrestrial broadcasting and placed under direct government control.

1981: Hosni Mubarak succeeds Sadat after Sadat's assassination. Emergency law, already in force since 1967, is enforced and renewed repeatedly until 2012.

1985: Egyptian Organisation for Human Rights is founded but denied a legal licence, which impedes local fund-raising; Arab Organisation of Human Rights gives it support in kind.

1990: Egypt uses Arabsat to transmit entertainment to its troops stationed in the Gulf, as part of the US-led coalition that ends Iraq's occupation of Kuwait in 1991.

1998: Egypt launches its own satellite, Nilesat.

1999: Saudi-owned satellite network Orbit launches an evening magazine and talkshow called *Cairo Today* from its Cairo studio, setting precedents that Egyptian channels will later follow.

2000: Egypt creates a Media Free Zone by decree and opens it to privately owned Egyptian broadcasters who accept transmitting by satellite and other editorial constraints.

2002: Culpability for a train fire that kills more than 370 passengers is discussed on a private TV channel.

2004: The Kefaya (Enough) movement is launched to oppose political corruption and a further presidential term for Hosni Mubarak or the transfer of power to his son Gamal.

2005: Egypt's constitution is amended to allow other candidates to compete with Mubarak for the presidency in that year's presidential election.

HISTORICAL BACKGROUND

2006: More than 1,000 Egyptians are drowned when a ferry of questionable seaworthiness sinks in the Red Sea, causing questions about corruption in high places to be aired in the private media.

2008: April 6 Youth Movement uses Facebook and Twitter to mobilise support for a workers' strike.

2010: Two policemen beat internet user Khaled Said to death in Alexandria in June, triggering widespread protests and calls for the interior minister to resign. Media clampdown precedes the November parliamentary elections, seen as the most fraudulent ever.

2011: 25 January revolution topples Mubarak on 11 February; the Supreme Council of the Armed Forces (SCAF) takes over; March referendum accepts limited constitutional amendments; parliamentary elections begin in November, creating a People's Assembly heavily dominated by the Muslim Brothers' Freedom and Justice Party (FJP) and the Salafist Nour Party.

2012: Parliament begins sessions in January but is dissolved by the Supreme Constitutional Court in June; first civilian president, Mohammed Morsi, elected in June, appears to assert his authority over SCAF in August through negotiation and sackings; Morsi's FJP supporters act to quell media voices raised against the Muslim Brotherhood.

Guide to Egyptian Media Outlets Mentioned in the Report

25TV: Youth-oriented TV channel launched 2011

Al-Ahram (The Pyramids): Daily newspaper founded 1875, state-run since 1960, has online/English versions

Al-Akhbar (The News): Daily newspaper founded 1952, state-run since 1960, has online/English versions

Akhbar al-Youm (News of the Day): Weekly newspaper founded 1944, state-run since 1960

Arabist.net: News blog collective

Aswat Masriya (Egyptian Voices): Thomson Reuters Foundation bilingual news project

Al-Badeel (The Alternative): Privately owned newspaper launched 2007

Banat wa Bas (Girls Only): Internet radio launched 2007

Bikya Masr (*bikya* = Egyptian term for 'resellable clutter', from the Italian *vecchia*): News website

CBC (Capital Broadcasting Centre): Private commercial TV channel launched 2011

Daily News Egypt: English-language newspaper and website launched 2005, closed and reopened under new owners 2012

El-Destour (The Constitution): Non-government newspaper launched 1995, banned 1998–2004, sold to Wafd Party businessmen 2010

Dream TV: Private commercial TV channel launched 2001

Egypt Independent: English-language sister paper to Al-Masry al-Youm

Egypt Monocle: Collective news blog launched 2012 by former staff of Daily News Egypt

ERTU (Egyptian Radio & Television Union): State-run broadcaster

Al-Fagr (Dawn): Privately owned newspaper launched 2005

Al-Fara'een (The Pharaohs): Private commercial TV channel launched 2010

Al-Ghad (Tomorrow): Al-Ghad Party newspaper, launched 2005

El-Gomhoreya (The Republic): Internet TV channel

Al-Gumhuriya (The Republic): Daily newspaper founded 1954, state-run since 1960

Al-Hayat (Life): Private commercial TV channel launched 2008
Hoqook (Rights): Internet radio and website launched 2010 to promote accurate reporting and human rights
Horytna (Our Freedom): Youth-oriented internet radio launched 2007
Masrawy.com (The Egyptian): Egyptian portal
Al-Masry al-Youm (The Egyptian Today): Privately owned newspaper launched 2004
Mayadeen Masr ([Town] Squares/spheres of Egypt) News Network: Online news service launched 2011
El-Mehwar (The Axis): Private commercial TV station launched 2002
Misr25 (Egypt 25): TV channel of Muslim Brotherhood launched 2011
Mosireen (Those who insist): Non-profit website and YouTube channel for citizen journalism and civic activism
Al-Nahar (Daylight) TV: Private commercial TV channel launched 2011
ONTV: Private commercial TV channel launched 2008
Rassd (acronym formed from words for 'watch, film, blog'): Online news service launched 2010
Sawt al-Shaab (Voice of the People): Parliamentary channel launched 2012
Sawt al-Umma (Voice of the Nation): Privately owned newspaper founded 1984, suspended 1994–2000
Al-Shorouk (Sunrise): Privately owned newspaper launched 2009
Tahrir (Liberation) TV: Private commercial channel launched 2011, changed hands 2011
Al-Tahrir (Liberation): Privately owned newspaper launched 2011
Al-Tarik (The Way): Coptic television station
Al-Wafd (The Delegation): New Wafd Party newspaper, established 1984 after one-party system ended in late 1970s
Al-Watan (The Homeland): Privately owned newspaper launched 2011
Al-Youm al-Sabea (Seventh Day): Privately owned newspaper launched 2008

Names and Positions of Some Egyptian Journalists and Bloggers Mentioned in the Report

Abbas, Wael	Blogger, Misrdigital and Al-Wa'ey al-Masri (Egyptian Awareness) blogs
Abdel-Fattah, Ahmad	Cameraman, *Al-Masry al-Youm*, shot in the eye by police, Nov. 2011
Abdel-Fattah, Alaa	Blogger, jailed Oct.–Dec. 2011
Abdel-Ghani, Hussein	Presenter, Al-Nahar TV; former Al-Jazeera Cairo bureau chief
Abdel-Rahman, Dina	Presenter, CBC; former presenter, Dream TV; former presenter, Tahrir TV
Al-Arabi, Mohammed	Reporter, Horytna Radio
Amin, Shahira	Former deputy head, Nile TV
Azab, Rasha	Reporter, *Al-Fagr*
Al-Daba, Mohammed	Journalist, *Sawt al-Umma*
Daniel, Meena	Blogger and member of Youth Movement for Freedom and Justice, killed in Maspero protest, Oct. 2011
El-Demerdash, Moataz	Presenter, Al-Hayat TV; former presenter, El-Mehwar
Eissa, Ibrahim	Editor, *Al-Tahrir*; former editor, *El-Destour*
Fadl, Bilal	Columnist and TV presenter
Fouda, Yosri	Presenter, ONTV; former Al-Jazeera investigative journalist
Galad, Magdi	Editor, *Al-Watan*; former editor, *Al-Masry al-Youm*
Ghanem, Yehia	Board chairman, Dar el-Helal; former journalist, *Al-Ahram*
Ghurab, Hazem	Director, Misr25
El-Hadidi, Lamis	Presenter, CBC
El-Hamalawy, Hossam	Blogger, 3arabawy.org
Hammamou, Sabah	Deputy business editor, *Al-Ahram*; video blogger
Hammouda, Adel	Editor, *Al-Fagr*
Hashish, Hala	Head of Nile Thematic Channels, ERTU
Ibrashi, Wael	Editor, *Sawt al-Umma*

El-Kahky, Amr	Cairo bureau chief, Al-Jazeera English
Kamel, Bouthaina	Broadcaster, formerly with Orbit TV and Egypt Radio
Kandil, Hamdi	Veteran print journalist and broadcaster
Al-Khafagy, Amr	Editor, *Al-Shorouk*; presenter, ONTV
Al-Laithy, Amr	Presenter, El-Mehwar; former presenter, Dream TV
Magdi, Rasha	Presenter, Egypt TV
Maged, Reem	Presenter, ONTV
Mahmoud, Ahmad	Journalist, *Al-Ta'awun* (Al-Ahram Foundation), shot by police 29 Jan. 2011, died 4 Feb. 2011
Al-Malky, Rania	Former editor, *Daily News Egypt*
El-Menawy, Abdel-Latif	Former head of news, ERTU
Mikhail, Wael	Reporter, Al-Tarik TV, killed in Maspero protest, Oct. 2011
Al-Mirazi, Hafez	Presenter, Dream TV; Director, Adham Centre for Television and Digital Journalism; former Al-Jazeera Washington bureau chief
Al-Mislimani, Ahmad	Presenter, Dream TV
Moheyldin, Ayman	Correspondent, NBC; former reporter for Al-Jazeera English
Moussa, Ahmad	Deputy chief editor, *Al-Ahram*
Negm, Nawara	Blogger, *Gabhit al-Tahyis al-Shaabiyya* (Popular Silliness Front)
Rizk, Yasser	Editor, *Al-Masry al-Youm*; former editor, *Al-Akhbar*
Saad, Mahmoud	Presenter, Al-Nahar TV; former presenter, Egypt TV
Saadi, Abeer	Secretary general and head of training, Journalists Syndicate
Saleh, Khaled	Editor, *Al-Youm al-Sabea*
Sanad, Maikel Nabil	Blogger, jailed Apr. 2011 for insulting army; released Jan. 2012
El-Sayyad, Sherine	Presenter, 25TV
Shazli, Mona	Presenter, Dream TV, June 2005–Sept. 2012, when she moved to Saudi-owned MBC Egypt channel, MBC Misr
Shukrallah, Hani	Editor, *AhramOnline*; former editor, *Al-Ahram Weekly*
Sarhan, Hala	Presenter, Rotana Misr TV; former presenter, Dream TV
El-Taweel, Bahaa	Producer, ONTV; former reporter, *Al-Youm al-Sabea*
El-Tunisy, Amani	Director, Banat wa Bas Radio
El-Waly, Mamdouh	Board Chairman, Al-Ahram (appointed Sept. 2012); Chair, Journalists Syndicate (elected Oct. 2011)
El-Wardani, Lina	Reporter, *Ahram Online*
Yehia, Karem	Journalist, *Al-Ahram*; founder of Journalists for Change
Younis, Nora	Multimedia Desk Editor, *Al-Masry al-Youm*; former blogger
Al-Zayat, Yasser	Journalism trainer and deputy editor, *Al-Izaa wa'l-telefiziyun* (Radio and TV)

1

A National Rethink of News Values

> Repression of journalists persisted after Mubarak's overthrow, partly as a reaction to the inventiveness of a growing spectrum of practitioners in the gathering and dissemination of news. This chapter traces multiple dimensions of both the repression and inventiveness.

What it means to be a journalist became a burning question during the events that toppled Egypt's President Mubarak on 11 February 2011. Unpaid news reporting was suddenly the order of the day as Egyptians without professional journalistic credentials spread images and information that were deliberately blocked or distorted inside the country's formal media institutions. As the British-Egyptian actor Khaled Abdalla put it later, this was one of the first revolutions in history to be 'filmed by its people rather than by a news organisation',[1] because normally well-resourced news providers relied on amateur cameraphone footage uploaded to YouTube and updates from Twitter.

During the early days of the uprising, government-run television channels avoided all shots of demonstrations and denied reports of the protests carried by the pan-Arab news channels, Al-Jazeera and Al-Arabiya. On 3 February, the day after men with swords and machetes rode horses and camels through crowds of protestors in Tahrir Square, and paving stones were thrown at protestors from the tops of buildings, government-run newspapers were still in denial. For *Al-Ahram*, the millions in the square had come to support Mubarak, while *Al-Akhbar*'s main headline alleged a huge 'conspiracy' against Egypt. Yet the independent *Al-Masry al-Youm* gave the lie to such official versions by reporting that Tahrir Square had become a battlefield.

CNN's Eliot Spitzer asked Egyptian journalist Ethar el-Katatney on air that evening how the Egyptian public felt about the stark contrast in coverage. She replied that Egyptians have long been accustomed to discounting what they call *kalam geraid* (newspaper speak), tolerating government propaganda for the sake of political stability.² At that moment, however, it seemed to many observers – practitioners inside and outside Egyptian government media institutions, and media freedom advocates, local and foreign – that journalism in Egypt had reached a tipping point, beyond which the public would insist on different news values from those espoused by editors working on a despised government's behalf.

In particular, lies about the so-called 'battle of the camel' and the protestors' demands caused fury among reporters inside the government media machine. Their fury added to the uprising's momentum. According to Salah Abdel-Maqsoud, who was soon to become temporary head of the Egyptian Journalists' Syndicate and later information minister, a 'steady stream' of 'presenters, producers, writers, columnists, commentators and technicians' walked away from their jobs in newspapers, news agencies, television, and radio.³ Shahira Amin famously left her post as deputy head of Nile TV, declaring on Al-Jazeera English that, despite working for Egyptian television since 1989 and receiving regular threats from state security in connection with her work, she had never before found herself complicit with broadcasting outright untruths. Suha al-Naqash, a Nile News anchor with 20 years' service, also walked out. She told AFP that she had been forced to report that Cairo streets were calm when, as she described it, the country was actually 'boiling over'.⁴

For several years the steps of Cairo's iconic and imposing Journalists' Syndicate building had served as an informal platform for voicing political dissent against the Mubarak regime. On 7 February 2011, around 1,000 journalists chose that venue to stage a symbolic funeral in protest at the killing of *Al-Ahram* employee Ahmad Mahmoud, who was shot by a member of the government's 'security' forces while photographing their clashes with demonstrators. *Al-Ahram*, whose online reporter Lina El-Wardani had already been assaulted and arrested by police on 26 January,⁵ revealed in its online English-language edition that the fatal shooting of Mahmoud was captured on cameraphone by seven eyewitnesses. Mahmoud had to be taken to hospital by colleagues because the ambulance service refused to respond when they heard that the injury was a bullet wound.⁶

The protest ended with a march to Tahrir Square and a speech from Inas Abdel-Alim, Mahmoud's wife, herself a journalist with *Al-Akhbar*. With other reporters having also come under attack from government forces, Journalists' Syndicate members threatened a vote of no confidence against the Syndicate's president, Makram Mohammed Ahmad, for deriding the protestors and failing to stand up to the Mubarak regime. When Mubarak finally fell, expectations of a new start for journalists were voiced officially. Ahmad Moussa, deputy chief editor of *Al-Ahram*, predicted that the ceiling of freedom for the press and other media would 'never be lowered again'. He said: 'We are all free now.'[7]

Today it is widely known that, contrary to Moussa's prediction, threats to free speech in Egypt not only persisted but intensified after the uprising. According to the Reporters sans Frontières (RSF) index, Egypt ranked 166 out of 179 countries in the first 11 months of 2011, down from 127 out of 178 countries in 2010.[8] As RSF recounted in November 2011, this was largely due to political continuity, whereby Mubarak's 'bloody crackdown' in February was perpetuated by the Supreme Council of the Armed Forces (SCAF), which 'not only retained Mubarak's methods of controlling the flow of information but made them even tougher'.[9] As a result, the overthrow of Mubarak in February was not the only period of exceptional violence against journalists in Egypt in 2011; it was followed by others in October, November, and December, and more still in 2012.

Political and military leaders' hostility to free expression does not tell the whole story, however. The RSF indices themselves acknowledge journalists' irrepressible urge to investigate and criticise. Thus a distinction exists to be made between two dimensions of the media landscape after the uprising. On the one hand are the harsh political power realities of the Mubarak–SCAF–Morsi transition and their impact on media institutions. On the other are challenges mounted by many different kinds of news reporters, paid and unpaid, not only to the political status quo but, more fundamentally, to the social order in media institutions and beyond.

Such challenges, as Jack Shenker pointed out for the *Guardian* during Egypt's presidential elections in 2012, cannot readily be gauged by a 'metric of revolutionary success', which is limited to the 'formal arena of institutional politics' or protests on Facebook or in Tahrir Square. 'In reality', Shenker argued, 'the purview of Egypt's revolution is far wider'. It reflects a grassroots 'struggle for real agency', which resonates with protest movements in parts of Europe in terms of the 'existential challenge' it poses to current systems of political and economic control.[10] The present report draws on that analysis for its rationale. A study of Egyptian journalism at this moment is justified because the 'struggle for real agency' is as evident in the sphere of news-gathering and dissemination as in other fields of Egyptian life.

The remainder of this chapter deals with the two dimensions of the media landscape mentioned above. The first section charts various facets of a brutal clampdown on journalists and bloggers during 2011–12. The second shifts the focus to a few reconfigurations of journalism that promised to outlast, or possibly even help to overcome, the multiple factors that prolonged Egypt's low press freedom score after the downfall of Mubarak. Both sections identify individuals and events with a certain amount of detail in terms of names and dates. The aim is to paint a sufficiently intimate picture for the subsequent chapters to be able to carry separate strands of the story forward without excess baggage of scene-setting and description.

It should be noted that, despite the attention paid to personalities and chronology in this chapter, there is no intention to construct a detailed timeline of the kind already available in publications such as *Jadaliyya* and *Al-Ahram Weekly*.[11] Instead, the purpose is to trace institutional, legal, judicial, physical, and moral forms of coercion of media practitioners, since distinctions between these forms are important for strands of analysis throughout the report. In the section on the re-energised news sector the aim is to compare and contrast start-ups and initiatives in terms of their contribution to amplifying and diversifying news coverage.

Intensified repression of the media under SCAF

In the immediate aftermath of Mubarak's removal on 11 February, there were hopes that a clean sweep of regime personnel would remove the heads of media institutions and the old regulatory framework. One of the first media officials to go, on 22 February, was the Journalists' Syndicate president, Makram Mohammed Ahmad, along with the chairman and editor-in-chief of *Al-Gumhuriya*, traditionally the most subservient of all the government-owned newspapers. Two days later came the arrest of Mubarak's minister of information, Anas el-Fiqi, and Osama el-Sheikh, director of the state broadcaster, the Egyptian Radio and Television Union (ERTU), on charges of profiteering and squandering public funds. It was no surprise that the two were charged together since the ERTU had always come under direct information ministry control. El-Fiqi had an office on the ninth floor of the ERTU building. He and El-Sheikh were later convicted and, initially, given prison sentences of seven and five years respectively.

A NATIONAL RETHINK OF NEWS VALUES

A similar fate befell Safwat Sharif, a top adviser to Mubarak's ruling party, the NDP, who had held the information ministry from 1981 to 2004; he was initially banned from travelling, then charged with illegal profiteering, and in July 2011 referred to a criminal court to face murder charges in connection with the 'battle of the camel'. For a few weeks from 7 March, when the cabinet of Prime Minister Essam Sharaf was sworn in and the information ministry was briefly abolished, Egypt joined the ranks of the very few Arab countries – Morocco, Qatar, UAE – with no such ministry.

The experience was shortlived. Thereafter, expectations of a radical overhaul of the media sector dissipated. In July a court cleared El-Fiqi of corruption and released El-Sheikh pending a hearing on a lesser charge. After installing an airforce general, Tarik al-Mahdi, as ERTU head to replace El-Sheikh, SCAF reinstated the information ministry on 9 July, appointing people close to the military as ministers. Their first choice was Osama Heikal, former military correspondent and editor of *Al-Wafd*, the organ of the Wafd Party, one of the few tame opposition parties allowed under Mubarak. On the eve of the uprising, Heikal had urged the government in an editorial to introduce rapid reform in order to avert a violent confrontation or repetition of what had happened in Tunisia.[12]

Heikal lasted in the post until late November, despite calls for his resignation after the events of 9 October when many independent journalists blamed his links to SCAF for ERTU misreporting of deadly clashes between the army and Coptic Christian demonstrators. Copts, angry at the demolition of a church, marched on the ERTU's Maspero headquarters. ERTU staff inside the building reported that soldiers had been injured by Coptic demonstrators[13] and a studio presenter, Rasha Magdi, gave a prolonged and histrionic monologue praising the army, whom she described as under attack and in need of defence by the Egyptian people. After 27 people died in the violence, cameraphone footage showed that a number had been run down by armoured personnel carriers. The ERTU's performance during the incident provoked a public outcry and a rebuke from the European Broadcasting Union (EBU), to which it belongs.[14] Magdi's personal contribution attracted fierce criticism in talkshows on two privately owned news channels, Dream 2 and ONTV.

When Heikal eventually resigned he did so along with the rest of Essam Sharaf's cabinet on 21 November, in the wake of another round of violent clashes between security forces and protesters. These clashes, near Mohamed Mahmoud Street in central Cairo, killed 43 people and, according to a joint press release issued by five Egyptian human rights organisations on 22 November, injured more than 2,000. The human rights organisations announced in the press release that they intended to prosecute named military figures, whom they held responsible for the 'brutal attacks on demonstrators' and liable, if they were not tried in Egypt, to be prosecuted by international courts. It noted that the attacks had been 'extensively documented' by the media and that the board of the Journalists' Syndicate had complained to the public prosecutor about deliberate attacks on journalists, leading to serious injuries.

The press release denounced military officials' 'fallacious statements' to the media and ended by insisting that 'all those responsible for the state media must be replaced'.[15] SCAF's choice of replacements for Sharaf and his ministers squarely rebuffed any call for renewal. The new prime minister, Kamal Ganzouri, aged 78 at the time of his appointment, had served three years in the same post under Mubarak in the 1990s. Ganzouri's information minister, Ahmad Anis, a retired major general who had previously headed the armed forces' Department for Army Morale, chaired the ERTU Board of Trustees when Anas el-Fiqi held the information ministry. Anis and El-Fiqi were reportedly very close.

At the ERTU itself, old faces remained in dominant positions. Major General Tarik al-Mahdi stayed at Maspero for a month, handing over to academic Sami Sherif, known for his close connections to Mubarak's ruling National Democratic Party, who himself left at the end of May 2011. Sherif was replaced by his deputy, Tharwat Mekki, initially in an acting capacity and then with a confirmed appointment in October. Mekki was the ERTU manager held responsible by many for delaying ERTU coverage of a bombing in Cairo's Khan el-Khalili tourist bazaar in April 2005. The ERTU's small report on the bombing, aired hours after it was covered by pan-Arab channels, relied on pictures from the Saudi-owned network MBC. *Al-Masry al-Youm*, which investigated the delay, found that Mekki's mobile phone had been switched off, leaving journalists without authorisation to report the event.

Further demonstrating the continuity in media repression before and after Mubarak, the state of emergency law, in force since 1981, remained on the statute books throughout 2011, empowering the Interior Ministry to detain people indefinitely without trial or charge. SCAF had recourse to the emergency law in April 2011 to reinforce a ban on strikes and sit-ins.[16] In September 2011 it renewed the law until the end of May 2012 and used it as the default framework for a crackdown on the press. On

11 September, police raided the office of Al-Jazeera Mubasher Misr, the Doha-based broadcaster's specialist channel for live coverage of Egypt,[17] and the channel was taken off air until it could shift transmission from Egypt to Qatar. The raid, allegedly triggered because Al-Jazeera Mubasher Misr was operating without a licence, was more or less a repeat of what had happened to the channel on 30 January, during the last days of Mubarak.

The fact that the raid had little to do with licensing (Al-Jazeera had applied for a licence extension on 20 March and been advised by the authorities to continue broadcasting) and much to do with content was implicitly acknowledged when SCAF announced the same day that it would be using the emergency law to punish 'threats to public order' caused by the dissemination of 'false information'. September also saw SCAF confiscating an edition of the independent weekly *Sawt al-Umma* after it criticised the General Intelligence Services for failing to release footage of Tahrir Square filmed by CCTV cameras on the Egyptian museum during the 18-day uprising.

In the second half of 2011 and early months of 2012, Egypt's military authorities tightened the legal squeeze not only on media institutions but also on individual journalists. This process started in May 2011, when ONTV presenter Reem Maged and blogger Hossam El-Hamalawy were ordered to appear before military judges after discussing video evidence of violations against protestors on an episode of Maged's current affairs talkshow *Baladna bil-Masry*.[18] ONTV's Nabil Sharafeddin was also called to the prosecutor's office after discussing theories that SCAF and the Muslim Brotherhood had agreed to share power. In June a military prosecutor interrogated *Al-Fagr* editor Adel Hammouda and journalist Rasha Azab for five hours, accusing them of endangering public security through 'false information' in an article about military police abuse of demonstrators, including forced virginity tests. In October, Mohammed al-Daba, working for *Sawt al-Umma*, investigated allegations of nepotism behind the award of a university post to the son of SCAF member General Mamdouh Shaheen. He received a military summons but, with the backing of his editor and the Journalists' Syndicate, refused to attend.[19]

By this time, however, it had become clear that, just as Mubarak had incarcerated media practitioners, his successors were ready to do the same. In mid-October a military appeals court ordered a retrial of Maikel Nabil Sanad, a 26-year-old blogger who had been imprisoned in April after being found guilty of 'insulting the Egyptian army' because of a blog post questioning unity between the army and the people. Sanad, on hunger strike, boycotted the retrial, which again took the form of a military tribunal and, after repeated postponements, merely reduced his prison sentence from three years to two.[20] His case highlighted SCAF's use of military courts to try civilians, which the campaign 'No to Military Trials of Civilians' estimated happened 12,000 times in 2011 alone, compared with 2,000 cases throughout the entire Mubarak presidency.

When internationally renowned blogger Alaa Abdel-Fattah was arrested at the end of October, charged with incitement during the Maspero clashes earlier that month, he refused to answer questions in a military court and was immediately jailed, where he remained for nearly two months. Like the raid on Al-Jazeera Mubasher Misr, this was another throwback to the Mubarak era, since Abdel-Fattah had spent 45 days in prison in 2006 after demonstrating in support of an independent judiciary. Under SCAF, Abdel-Fattah was accused of inciting attacks on soldiers, stealing a military weapon, and destroying military property. Since the charges were plainly absurd, it was widely assumed that his real offence in the eyes of the military was to have contributed an article to the Egyptian daily, *Al-Shorouk*, about the killing of 25-year-old anti-sectarian activist and blogger Meena Daniel during the Maspero protest on 9 October. Abdel-Fattah's article described how Daniel's supporters had pressed for autopsies for Daniel and the other deceased.

Daniel was one of two known media practitioners among the fatalities in Maspero, the second being Wael Mikhail, a reporter for the Coptic television station Al-Tarik. Physical attacks on the media escalated from that point. On the evening of 9 October, military police stormed the premises of two private TV stations located near Maspero, which were broadcasting live footage of the clashes that contradicted the ERTU version of events. The stations, Egyptian channel 25TV, run by young people in their 20s, and US-owned Al-Hurra, were forced off air. Some staff at 25TV, including news presenter Sherine El-Sayyad, who was pregnant, reported that they were physically assaulted.[21] Viewers receiving the 25TV broadcast at the time of the raid heard screams.

Targeted attacks continued during the Mohamed Mahmoud Street clashes in November, prompting the Journalists' Syndicate to lodge a formal complaint, as noted above. According to information relayed by the Syndicate to the Committee to Protect Journalists (CPJ), at least 17 assaults on the press, including beatings in custody and shootings, were counted in Cairo and Alexandria in November in the space of two days. Apart from an injury sustained by one person from Egypt's Middle East News Agency

(MENA), all other locally employed victims worked for non-government outlets. Four of the injured worked for *Al-Masry al-Youm*, three for *Al-Shorouk*, two for *Al-Youm al-Sabea*, one for *Al-Fagr*, one for the Lebanese daily *Al-Akhbar*, and three for *Al-Tahrir*, a newspaper created after the uprising. Of the remaining two, one edited a youth website and the other was a freelance photographer.[22] Ahmad Abdel-Fattah, a photojournalist with *Al-Masry al-Youm*, lost an eye. He said policemen aimed at his eyes and at anyone holding a camera.[23]

In the final analysis, CPJ counted 35 cases of journalists being attacked on 19–24 November, including several brutal attacks carried out by non-uniformed assailants and some targeted at internationally known figures.[24] Less than one month later, almost immediately after the second round of parliamentary elections ended, a further five days of clashes occurred. They were sparked on 16 December, when security forces tried to evict protestors from in front of the Cabinet Office, where they were staging a sit-in against the appointment of Ganzouri. Despite efforts by newly elected MPs and parliamentary candidates to broker a truce, the toll in that round of violence reached an estimated 16 dead, with 928 injured.[25]

This time, CPJ reported at least 15 attacks on the press, mostly by uniformed soldiers beating reporters and destroying equipment.[26] Media coverage, reminiscent of the 18-day uprising in Tahrir, split into those outlets determined to report what they saw and those, like *Al-Ahram*, which shunned pictures of soldiers and police in action and blamed the violence on others, in this case drug addicts, street children, ex-convicts, and football hooligans.[27] Journalists in the government-controlled media who dared to discuss army violence, like radio presenters Ziad Ali and Nermeen El-Banbi, lost their slots.[28]

On 17 December, at the height of the clashes, a group of military police were seen dragging a woman on the ground by her outer garments, exposing her partially naked body and blue bra, and stamping on her torso. The sequence, captured in video and a still image, was published on the front pages of non-government newspapers such as *Al-Shorouk* and *Al-Tahrir*, the latter emblazoning the picture with the single word *Kazeboon* (Liars) in reference to SCAF denials of excessive or targeted force. The woman in the picture, 28-year-old Ghada Kamel, an activist with the April 6 movement – originally formed to mobilise for strike action in 2008 – recorded her testimony for BBC Arabic and Mosireen, an Egyptian non-profit media collective that launched a YouTube channel dedicated to such accounts.[29]

The responses of SCAF and its associates to the December events seemed to be aimed at, among other things, discrediting non-government media by alleging that they were working to a suspicious agenda. Retired General Abdel-Moneim Kato, an adviser to the Armed Forces Department for Army Morale, stated in *Al-Shorouk* that the forces' treatment of protestors was 'appropriate' and he accused the media of clinging to the 'tiniest details without offering to solve the problem'. He continued: 'We're all watching Egypt and its history burn, and you're concerned over some street bully who deserves to be thrown into Hitler's ovens'.[30] According to Kato the clashes were incited by people with 'foreign agendas' and satellite channels were deliberately trying to damage the army's reputation.[31]

Kato's insinuation of a link between journalists and foreign interests repeated a line of propaganda familiar under Mubarak. On 1 February 2011, the privately owned channel El-Mehwar had memorably interviewed a 'former journalist' identified only as Shaimaa, who claimed that she and other demonstrators in Tahrir had received free training from Israelis in Qatar (home of Al-Jazeera) and the USA on how to overthrow dictators. The fear-mongering continued under SCAF. Ilan Grapel, a US-Israeli visitor to Egypt who had publicised his presence in the country on Facebook, was arrested in June 2011 on spying charges and eventually held for five months. State-run newspapers splashed allegations taken verbatim from security sources that he had been emailing reports from internet cafés to the Israeli intelligence agency Mossad.

The lurid coverage prompted bloggers and one or two independent newspapers to accuse SCAF of trying to drum up nationalist paranoia in order to deflect criticism from itself. But the campaign of sowing suspicion continued. In June 2012 a 40-second advertisement, linking foreigners, journalism, and treachery ran on state television and, briefly, private channels. Titled 'A word saves a nation', the clip showed an English-speaking foreigner discussing politics with three Egyptian youths in a café and then apparently conveying the contents of his conversation on his mobile phone.[32] It was part of a series that also warned Egyptians against sharing information online, for fear it could be used by foreign spies.[33]

One year on from 25 January 2011 the climate in Egypt for progressive journalism seemed to be deteriorating almost by the day. SCAF's head, Field-Marshal Tantawi, announced on the eve of the first anniversary of the uprising that the emergency law would be lifted with effect from 25 January 2012, except for cases of what he described, with no further amplification, as thuggery (*baltagiya*). Yet when the law formally expired at the end of May, the Justice Ministry tried to revive it by authorising military personnel to arrest civilians without a warrant. At the moment of Mohammed Morsi's swearing in as president, on 30 June, legal challenges were under way against this and numerous other measures, including the dissolution of Parliament and SCAF's supplementary constitutional declaration entrenching and widening its powers. SCAF's actions throughout 2011 and into 2012 were far from observing Egypt's commitment to international human rights conventions guaranteeing journalists' right to report.

In early February 2012, according to CPJ monitoring, there were ten attacks on the press over a four-day period, after 72 people were killed in Port Said, seemingly over a football match. Few people believed football to be the reason for violence erupting, since it was supporters of the winning team who attacked the losing team with weapons that should never have been allowed near the pitch, while security forces looked on. Al-Ahly Ultras, supporters of the losing team, were no ordinary football fans: they had become known for their part in anti-regime protests. In the ensuing demonstrations at lack of security in the stadium and continued military rule, journalists filming in Suez were beaten and their cameras broken by attackers in civilian clothes. The CPJ accounts record that they were denied legal redress. Others filming in Cairo were shot with pellets[34] by state security forces.

As previously, the majority affected worked for non-government outlets. This time they included *Al-Masry al-Youm*, TV stations ONTV and CBC, Jordan-based website *Al-Bawaba*, online newspaper *Al-Badeel* and online radio stations Horytna and Hoqook. However, one government-employed journalist, working for *Al-Akhbar*, was among those attacked in Suez, where injuries included a stabbed hand and two reporters said they were fired on. In Cairo, shotgun pellets injured the eye of state-run Nile TV's Mahmoud al-Ghazali and narrowly missed the eyes of Salma Said, filming for Mosireen.[35] *Al-Badeel*'s Mohammed Rabe'a was detained and reportedly beaten by police.

Major clashes erupted again on 2 May, near the Ministry of Defence in Abbassiya, Cairo, when the army moved against protestors angry at the disqualification of a Salafist leader from running in the presidential election. After some Salafist protestors were killed, 4 May saw a much bigger demonstration of solidarity with the Salafis by diverse groups. Uniformed and plain-clothes personnel used batons, live ammunition, and pellets to disperse the crowds; the death toll was 11, with hundreds injured and arrested, including 18 journalists. The worst injured, Mohammed Rafaat of Masrawy newsite, needed 25 stitches. Abdel-Rahman Yousef, photographer for Hoqook's website, lost part of his ear in a knife attack, and *Egypt Independent*'s photojournalist Virginie Nyugen was injured in the face. Five journalists for *Al-Watan* newspaper, only recently created, were beaten by police, hit by stones, or overcome by tear gas. Reporters for *Al-Masry al-Youm* and *Al-Badeel* were detained, as was the entire seven-man crew of the satellite broadcaster Misr25, some of whom said they were beaten by security forces.

The next day, 5 May, journalists held their own protest in front of the Journalists' Syndicate against the intensified repression of the past 15 months. Syndicate official Salah Abdel-Maqsoud deplored SCAF's treatment of those 'heroes' who were enabling people to exercise their legal right to know. 'Instead of celebrating World Press Freedom Day [3 May] we have these atrocities', he said, and called on political leaders to intervene to end them.³⁶ Less than three months later, on 2 August, Abdel-Maqsoud himself became information minister, as one of five Muslim Brothers appointed to the first cabinet of President Mohammed Morsi. Within a week, his own approach to media regulation was put to the test when two journalists entering a television studio at Media Production City complained of having been set upon by bearded protestors angry about the stridently anti-Islamist channel Al-Fara'een. A Muslim Brotherhood spokesman denied allegations of violence. Yet the government, acting through the state prosecutor, ordered Al-Fara'een off air and confiscated the 11 August edition of the daily newspaper *El-Destour*. It filed a lawsuit against Al-Fara'een's owner, Tawfik Okasha, whom it accused of insulting Morsi and inciting people to kill him, and another against Islam Afifi, the editor of *El-Destour*, whom it blamed for content highly critical of the Muslim Brotherhood.³⁷

A re-energised news sector

With its crackdown on media coverage of both military rule and protests against military rule, SCAF testified to the remarkable vitality and diversity of news-gathering in post-Mubarak Egypt. Growth in numbers and diversity of outlets is evident from the sequence of injuries and arrests between October 2011 and May 2012, recounted above, but the new-found vitality was more than a matter of quantity. NBC correspondent Ayman

Moheyldin, an Egyptian who covered the original Tahrir uprising for Al-Jazeera English, told a fellow journalist some months later that one of its fruits had been the 'new energy injected in Egyptian media'.[38]

Energy was far from lacking before the Mubarak–SCAF handover: certain journalists' persistent challenges to censorship were a key ingredient of the country's changing political dynamics, as parts of Chapter 2 will show. Several newspapers and television stations mentioned in the previous section helped to build up pressure against dysfunctional governance: from the 2004 launch of *Al-Masry al-Youm*, to the 2005 introduction of Dream TV's nightly current affairs show *Al-Ashera Masa'an* (10pm); from the 2007 launch of *Al-Badeel*'s shortlived paper version, to the arrival of ONTV's personable current affairs presenters in 2009. With Mubarak's removal, however, came a fresh surge in media initiatives and innovation.

As SCAF and the military insisted ever more strongly on protecting their budgets and extensive economic activities from scrutiny,[39] taking extreme measures to resist meaningful civilian oversight, so journalists and bloggers made it their business to translate the notion of civilian oversight into reality. One of the earliest examples on television came when Ahmad Shafik, the former airforce commander whom Mubarak appointed as prime minister on 29 January 2011, was confronted by veteran journalist and activist Hamdi Kandil and novelist Alaa al-Aswany during an ONTV talkshow on 2 March. Described as 'unforgettable' for viewers who had never before seen a prime minister being 'really interrogated and roasted',[40] the encounter took place when Shafik, unscathed by an appearance that evening on *Baladna bil-Masry*, agreed to stay in the studio for Yosri Fouda's *Akher Kalam* (Last Word) immediately afterwards. ONTV decided to join the two shows together and the channel's owner, Nagib Sawiris, who was soon to found the liberal Free Egyptians Party, also took part.

Despite attempts by the ONTV representatives to calm the exchanges and keep them on track, Shafik's angry refusal to give clear answers to questions about violence against protestors or the role of the country's 'security' forces put him increasingly on the defensive, and led him to gesticulate dismissively and even aggressively at times. Ignoring the common courtesies in Egyptian forms of address, Shafik shouted at Aswany with his first name, 'Ya Alaa, Ya Alaa',[41] telling him 'Ana bas befahimak al dunya mashya ezei' (I'm just making you understand how the world works) – a declaration that was not only insulting in itself, but exposed a failure to acknowledge that the whole point of the revolution was to make the Egyptian world work differently. Asserting that incidences of torture had nothing to do with him and that his previous record was irrelevant, Shafik insisted: 'Assess me from today.' Hours after the grilling, Shafik resigned.

Mona Shazli, host of Dream 2's *Al-Ashera Masa'an*, tackled three SCAF generals on 21 February 2011, with help from fellow journalist Wael Ibrashi, Revolutionary Youth Coalition member Shadi Ghazali Harb, and members of the public phoning in. She repeated the exercise eight months later, on 19 October, ten days after the Maspero killings. Together with Ibrahim Eissa, hardened survivor of countless censorship battles with the Mubarak regime and initiator of the newly created Tahrir TV and *Al-Tahrir* newspaper, Shazli plied two uniformed members of SCAF with questions, including many from the public, for three hours. The generals did not appreciate the ordeal, as indicated when one complained about the preponderance of critical comments from viewers.[42]

By October 2011 the Egyptian public was better equipped to question government representatives than ever before, thanks to at least three developments in sources of information. One was the access obtained to intelligence files from the notorious State Security Intelligence offices in early March, when protestors stormed around eight centres across the country in order to prevent the files from being destroyed. A significant amount of material was removed before the military secured the buildings and was duly uploaded to the internet. Blogger Hossam el-Hamalawy, who had himself been detained and tortured by State Security in 2000, posted pictures and details of intelligence officers he found in Nasr City headquarters in Cairo, but did not post the officers' family pictures, which he found in the same archive.[43]

Blogs and social media sites had played a significant part in supplying information and pictures to mainstream media and the public at large before the January uprising, because censorship of offline media under Mubarak turned cyberspace into the forum of last resort for Egyptians wanting to report freely. Online–offline collaborations became evident in 2006, when the production team of *Al-Ashera Masa'an* and some print outlets started to draw on information from blogs, including Hamalawy's, to investigate incidents of malpractice and torture by security forces. Interactions continued through the strikes and unrest of 2008 and the unprecedented public outcry at the brutal police killing of internet user Khaled Said in Alexandria in June 2010. A Facebook page, 'We Are All Khaled Said', administered anonymously by Google executive Wael Ghoneim, mobilised regular street demonstrations from then on. When, on 7 February 2011, Shazli interviewed Ghoneim minutes after his release from 12 days in secret police detention, her introduction indicated that Ghoneim had not been anonymous to the *Al-Ashera Masa'an* team.[44]

Online news sources spiralled after February 2011, spurred on in part by campaigns to capture and collate citizen journalism footage of violence and human rights abuse, but also by the shock of unsuspecting bystanders who suddenly found themselves witnessing brutality from a balcony or other vantage point with a cameraphone in their hands. Again, the orchestrated online gathering of evidence of abuse was not a new phenomenon. TV presenter Bouthaina Kamel, an early candidate for the post-Mubarak presidential election and one of the few people who challenged SCAF about virginity tests forced on female protestors, had used the internet to monitor vote rigging during the elections of 2005. She and two colleagues had set up a site called Shayfeen.com, a play on *shayfeenkum* (we see you).

In 2010 a group of students created a news site on Facebook and Twitter that was to become an important source for major global news providers during the events of early 2011. This was Rassd, later to become Rassd News Network, whose name encapsulates the practice of citizen journalism, since it stands for *rakeb* (observe), *sawwer* (film), and *dawwen* (blog). One of its founders says he was inspired by a training programme he attended in Egypt ahead of the 2010 elections,[45] aimed at improving the standards of citizen journalists and putting them in touch with professional journalists in mainstream media. The Washington-based International Centre for Journalists (ICFJ), which provided the programme, was later caught up in the Egyptian government's crackdown on civil society groups receiving US support (see Chapter 4). Rassd, meanwhile, having published videos of fraud and bullying during the 2010 elections, and survived government hacking and smear campaigns during the uprising, went on to expand its news operation, eventually facing competition from Mayadeen Masr News Network, set up by other activists with Twitter accounts.

Mosireen, the media collective already mentioned twice above because of its role in recording violence against activists, had its origins among filmmakers who congregated in the media tent in Tahrir Square in January–February 2011. It emerged as a workspace and YouTube channel some months later, after the Maspero killings, becoming the world's most-viewed non-profit YouTube channel during the month of January 2012. Mosireen's name plays on the Arabic word for Egyptians, which is written the same way but pronounced differently; the actual meaning of Mosireen is 'those who insist'. Its members describe their project as 'civic media', representing a 'different kind of journalism', which responds to the public's 'lack of faith' in state media or corporate structures and their 'demand' for alternative sources of information.[46]

Besides being posted online, Mosireen's collection of testimonies and footage of protests also reached the public directly on outdoor cinema screens. Achieving this involved cooperation with Kazeboon (Liars), an activist initiative intended to let the public see for themselves whether the official SCAF-endorsed version of events carried by state media tallied with what ordinary people's cameras and experiences showed. In setting up screenings in different locations in Cairo, the youth alliance behind Kazeboon learned how to go about disproving official accounts of street violence, which blamed it on foreign forces or the demonstrators themselves.

A third element in the proliferation of information sources was the rapid emergence of new television channels and newspapers, with their potential to amplify public awareness of amateur video. New television channels were the first to launch, by satellite because of the ERTU's continuing terrestrial monopoly; they joined the array of existing privately-owned satellite channels – Dream, El-Mehwar, ONTV, Al-Hayat, Al-Fara'een – the oldest of which (Dream, dating from late 2001) was still less than ten years old when Mubarak fell. All the existing channels belonged to businessmen who had grown rich under Mubarak and most had either played it safe or even supported the old regime. In the first months after the uprising, some new ventures differentiated themselves by claiming to represent 'the people', observe 'true' impartiality, or by following an innovative business model. With the passage of time, rich businessmen with financial power reasserted their influence. For a pivotal period, however, the volume, speed, and aspirations of start-ups injected a burst of energy into the mainstream media.

Ibrahim Eissa, a larger-than-life figure in dissident journalism, was one of three people who set up Tahrir TV on 8 February,[47] three days before Mubarak was removed. The colourful alliance behind the channel promoted it as coming 'from the nation to the nation' with the aim of 'liberating minds'. Eissa's partners were Ahmad Abu Haiba, with a track record in 'Islamic entertainment',[48] and an interior designer named Mohamed Mourad. They did not wait for a permit; Abu Haiba bypassed Egypt's state-owned satellite Nilesat and applied instead to Bahrain-based Noorsat, known for leasing frequencies to channels that had been dropped from Nilesat during the former ruling party's pre-election crackdown in 2010.

In its early days, Tahrir TV attracted prominent journalists who had done much to reveal the dire state of the country under the former regime. Among them were Bilal Fadl, known for his critical reporting in *Al-Masry al-Youm*, Amr al-Laithy, presenter of the interview programme *Wahed min al-Nas* (One of the People) on Dream 2, and Hamdi Kandil, broadcaster and newspaper columnist. The honeymoon did not last. Financial pressures prompted Eissa and his partners to seek other owners, with the result that, by the end of 2011, a large majority of shares had passed to Suleiman Amer, a businessman connected to the same regime whose corruption Tahrir's journalists had exposed. In the meantime, Eissa joined forces with Ibrahim Moallem, the chairman of *Al-Shorouk*, to create a newspaper called *Al-Tahrir*, separate from Tahrir TV. The paper's first edition, in July, featured a column by Bilal Fadl.

25TV followed Tahrir TV as a second independent television voice in April 2011. Its owner, long-established video entrepreneur Mohammed Gohar, recruited young staff from among activists in Tahrir Square, who had yet to be trained as journalists.[49] The project benefited from the regional infrastructure of Gohar's other company, Video Cairo Sat, the first private Egyptian source of television images to be allowed onto Nilesat at the end of the 1990s, and a supplier of footage from across Egypt to global news providers. 25TV reported from the Delta town of Mehalla on 6 April, thereby commemorating both an anniversary of the 2008 strikes and the origins of the Facebook-savvy April 6 youth movement.

Misr25, a general channel started by Egypt's Muslim Brotherhood in May, followed another model, based on donations from the faithful, supplemented by advertising. The venture drew its staff in part from former employees of Al-Jazeera or the Muslim Brotherhood website, ikhwanonline.com. Brotherhood officials were reported as specifying that they wanted media professionals with diverse backgrounds to represent a range of ideas. There were precedents for this approach. The 350 Egypt-based staff of the website IslamOnline, who staged a mass walkout from their workplace in March 2010 because of editorial changes imposed by the website's Qatari owners, included non-Muslims and non-practising Muslims. The Egyptian employees of IslamOnline had wanted to maintain the website's non-religious content.

Some generalist commercial channels entered the scene before and during Ramadan, the traditional high season for evening television viewing and advertising budgets, which in 2011 coincided with the month of August. Two of these, CBC (Capital Broadcasting Centre) and Al-Nahar TV, eventually came to share an owner, after CBC backer Mohammed Al-Amin Ragab, business partner of a property tycoon connected to the Mubarak family, acquired the majority of shares in Al-Nahar. Al-Nahar, managed by Samir Youssef, a producer of sports programmes and Mona Shazli's husband, recruited Hussein Abdel-Ghani, Al-Jazeera's former Cairo bureau chief. In May 2012, Al-Nahar partnered with France 24 to host successive nightly encounters with Egypt's presidential candidates.

CBC was quickly dubbed the channel of the 'remnants' (*feloul*) of the Mubarak regime because its presenters included Lamis el-Hadidi and, from February 2012, her brother-in-law Emad el-Din Adeeb. Both had made important media contributions to Mubarak's 2005 presidential election campaign. Other CBC figures were Abdullah Hammouda, previously associated with the government-run *Rose el-Yousef* magazine, and Magdi Galad of *Al-Masry al-Youm*. Although *Al-Masry al-Youm* gained a reputation for independence, Galad himself had previously intimated personal support for Gamal Mubarak. At the end of 2011, Galad played a part in blocking publication of the print version of the *Egypt Independent*, an English-language daily sister paper to *Al-Masry al-Youm*, because of one article, written by an American academic, which was deemed critical of SCAF. In March 2012, Galad resigned from *Al-Masry al-Youm* and took several of its staff members with him to a new paper paying higher salaries. This was *Al-Watan*, launched in late April 2011 under the ownership of CBC and Al-Nahar shareholder Mohammed Al-Amin.

It became much harder to start satellite channels after SCAF suspended licensing and cracked down on unlicensed operations in September 2011, although the parliamentary channel, Sawt al-Shaab (Voice of the People), did start to relay proceedings from the People's Assembly when MPs took their seats on 23 January 2012. After Parliament was dissolved six months later, Sawt al-Shaab applied to broadcast meetings of the Shura Council and Constituent Assembly. As demonstrated by what happened to the *Egypt Independent*, press start-ups also became difficult, while the economic downturn threatened some existing titles. In April 2012 the respected English-language *Daily News Egypt* faced closure after seven years in operation, following a dramatic slump in advertising sales and subscriptions during 2011. Its editor-in-chief Rania al-Malky and the rest of her team, unable to reach an accommodation on editorial independence with the new owner, created an online publication called *Egypt Monocle*. In contrast, *Al-Youm al-Sabea* (Seventh Day), an independent weekly started in 2008, went daily at the end of May 2011 and experimented briefly with an English-language version of its *Youm7* news website. Walid Mustafa, its publisher, also became a director of Al-Nahar TV.

Overview

Despite the ascendancy of Mubarak-era media owners in the private sector and despite the shift back towards ownership concentration behind the scenes, the sheer multiplication of different media spaces for reporting and comment on air, in print, and online made it much harder to marginalise individual journalists. Voices silenced in one space would instantly be heard in another, and attempts at censorship very quickly exposed. Colleagues from different media outlets would interview each other about their experience of repression and their aspirations for media freedom, reflecting a form of solidarity in tune with the mood of January 2011, as encapsulated in the name of the influential Facebook page, 'We are all Khaled Said'. Facebook afforded members of the public a means to express support for trusted journalists, as happened when Yosri Fouda announced in May 2012 that he would quit his programme to mark the scheduled 30 June return to civilian rule.

Revolutionary energy was no more easily contained in the news sector than elsewhere. Journalists clashed with each other over the best ways to represent their interests and with their bosses over journalistic standards and rights to free speech. The ERTU building became a site of permanent protest by staff seeking radical change. Superficial readings of the landslide outcome of elections to the People's Assembly and the eventual choice of president belied the diversity of sites of open contention and dissent. Headlines indicated a decisive win for Islamists in Parliament and a two-way presidential run-off between a Muslim Brotherhood candidate and a Mubarak appointee. Yet the number of votes for the Muslim Brothers' Freedom and Justice Party plummeted in just six months, from just over 10.1 million in the parliamentary elections in December 2011–January 2012 to less than 5.8 million for the Brotherhood candidate, Mohammed al-Morsi, in the first round of the presidential contest in May 2012.

In the same round, Hamdeen Sabahi, who came third overall with more than one-fifth of the total votes, was the clear winner out of the five candidates in five important governorates out of 27, namely Cairo,

Alexandria, Kafr al-Sheikh, Port Said, and Red Sea.[50] Sabahi, a founding member of the National Association for Change and a pro-labour activist, had joined the 25 January demonstrations from the first day. His Karama (Dignity) Party started as a breakaway from the Nasserite Party in the 1990s but was denied registration until August 2011. Sabahi's votes in the first round, added to those of the two other pro-revolution candidates, Abdel-Moneim Aboul-Futouh and Khaled Ali, accounted for 38.8 per cent of the total.

The fine balance of political forces may explain why Morsi, on finally announcing his largely technocratic cabinet at the beginning of August 2012, allocated only five portfolios (education, housing, labour, youth, and information) to known Muslim Brothers, while neglecting to recognise other political parties in assigning posts and actively sidelining the Salafist trend. Egypt's Muslim Brotherhood movement, having been prevented for decades from operating as a political party, came to power before having an opportunity to resolve its own internal divisions over central issues of governance, such as the state's role in the economy or its social responsibilities. In light of such divisions, many observers feared that staying in power could become an objective in itself, even if it entailed accommodations with vested military or business interests established before and during the Mubarak era. Thus the new information minister's background as a journalist who worked for Islamist publications, combined with the information ministry's continuing role in state broadcasting, failed to inspire hope that a Morsi government would resist the temptation to use state media as a tool of government.

In the post-Mubarak media landscape, however, voices opposing rule by the military, the Muslim Brotherhood, or vested interests from the Mubarak era, found ways to be heard. That landscape provides a backdrop for the analysis of competing visions of journalism attempted in the remaining chapters of this book.

2

Lessons from the Push for Professional Autonomy

> Decades of censorship – imposed through laws, intimidation and direct government control of giant press and broadcasting entities – thwarted the forging of a national consensus on norms of journalistic autonomy and objectivity. The trajectories of individual journalists and their wrangling with media owners and institutions, recalled in this chapter, reveal a wealth of professional experience and commitment, enthusiasm for cross-media collaboration with bloggers and social media users, and divergent approaches to what constitutes 'fair' reporting.

Egypt under Mubarak displayed a puzzling combination of authoritarian and liberal features, which caused some political scientists to label it a 'hybrid regime'.[1] Its media scene was undeniably enlivened by a range of privately owned outlets, several of which clearly decided their own editorial policies. Yet these coexisted with stifling controls, often exercised away from public view, including extrajudicial violence against journalists.[2] Elections took place but were organised to be uncompetitive, with deeply unfair media coverage of election campaigns. The constitution remained as a point of judicial reference and civil courts continued to function, while all the time the emergency law and security courts denied citizens their constitutional rights.[3] Theories of the hybrid regime held that it would remain stable for as long as cognitive dissonance between the trappings and realities of participatory politics could be obscured.[4]

Drawing on this analytical model and on dramatic developments in Egypt's press and politics since the launch of the Kefaya (Enough) opposition movement in 2004, Robert Springborg predicted in 2009 that the Mubarak government had sown the seeds of its own destruction. It had gambled that giving space for the expression of political thinking was not the same as allowing political action. It was consequently late in recognising the threat posed by the political counter-culture emerging online, in the blogosphere and elsewhere.⁵ Although such predictions of a tipping point were not unusual among scholars of the Egyptian scene in 2009,⁶ Springborg's particular insight was to note the centrality of conflicting perceptions of 'the word'. The Mubarak regime, having frequent resort to prison sentences, fines, and other coercive measures against journalists, apparently believed it possible to crush any challenge they posed. Journalists and bloggers disagreed.

A thoughtful analysis of Egypt's press, posted quasi-anonymously on the Baheyya blog at a moment when several newspaper editors were facing trial in September 2007, pinpointed a sea change in its content. Under the heading 'The Death of Deference', its author described the country's independent newspapers as more diverse and more 'systematically aggressive' than in any previous era. They were castigating the President on a far broader range of issues, she wrote, encompassing not only domestic and foreign policies but also the regime's own survival strategies, especially the presidential succession. This had come about because

> a new generation of journalists is at the helm. There's no uniformity among these journalists and they come from starkly different schools and backgrounds, but together they're a different breed from both the tame fare offered up by the old opposition press and the agitprop of the government newspapers. The new boldness in style is maintained by the mimicry and competition among the new papers: competition for readers, competition for ads, and competition for the social prestige that comes with being a bold regime critic and a good wordsmith.⁷

In 2011–12, deference to SCAF was in short supply. On 19 January 2012 the Wafd Party newspaper's online edition ran the headline 'Al-Shaab Yurid "Ra's" al-Mushir' (The People Demand the Field-Marshal's Head), echoing chants about the people's demands in Tahrir one year earlier. To avoid any ambiguity over that headline, a second immediately below it stated: 'Mubarak and Tantawi … same disappointment, same fate'. With such explicit taunting of the country's self-appointed leaders, it seemed unlikely that the gap between political expression and political action, so resoundingly closed as part of the dynamics that brought down the Mubarak regime, could be opened up again.

Yet fears of just such an outcome were implicit in worries that the generals would try to shield the army from civilian oversight by preserving a 'hybrid military-civilian deep state'.[8] Indeed, Article 196 of the Draft Constitution released in October 2012 even envisaged presenting the Armed Forces budget as a 'one-line item in the State budget',[9] although this was later removed. As noted in the blog post quoted above, Egypt's journalists hail from 'starkly different' schools and backgrounds. They include individuals who, for one reason or another, have been loyalists of the generals and prominent figures of the Mubarak era, and others who, because they work in state-owned media, regard themselves as government employees whose role is to produce complimentary publicity for the regime of the day, whether led by Mubarak, SCAF, or Morsi with military support. Others still may take a salary from government-run outlets while also writing or broadcasting elsewhere.

Egypt's journalists learned their craft in a context created by the particular evolution of the country's press during the latter part of the twentieth century and the particular evolution of its broadcasting sector during the twenty-first century. As will be shown, that evolution thwarted the development of a national consensus on professionalism, including the journalistic autonomy that is widely seen[10] as its key component. Pointers to the feasibility of narrowing the gaps between different approaches can only emerge from an exploration of the different attitudes and experiences of today's practising journalists.

Diverse approaches to the profession

Obstacles to a consensus on journalistic professionalism are a legacy of the 1960 nationalisation of newspapers under Nasser's one-party rule. The nationalisation, combined with Nasser's frequent jailing of prominent journalists, reflected his frustration at their lack of docility before and after the 1952 revolution. Ihsan Abdel-Quddous, editor of the outspoken *Rose el-Youssef* magazine founded by his mother, was jailed before the revolution for reporting that Egyptian troops fighting in Palestine were supplied with defective weapons. He was jailed again afterwards for writing an article about Nasser under the title 'The Secret Group that Rules Egypt'.[11]

Mustafa Amin, co-founder with his brother Ali of the daily *Al-Akhbar* and weekly *Akhbar al-Youm*, inspired by aspects of the American press,[12] was jailed by an emergency military court in 1965 on charges of spying for the USA. Amin later recounted that, under Nasser, every newspaper editor had been exiled, imprisoned, banned from writing, or sacked.¹³ Even Doria Shafik, founder and editor of two feminist magazines, was put under house arrest. The main exception was Nasser's civilian friend and confidant, Mohammed Hassanein Heikal, who was editor-in-chief of *Al-Ahram* for 17 years. But he too was to fall from grace when he differed with Nasser's successor, Sadat. Heikal was removed from *Al-Ahram*, banned from writing in Egyptian papers, and eventually jailed, shortly before Sadat's assassination in 1981. That was a period when Sadat imprisoned some 1,500–1,600 writers and politicians.

Nevertheless, in 1977, Sadat reintroduced political parties and allowed them to publish partisan newspapers. This created a clear dichotomy. On one side, government-controlled nationalised newspapers (*Al-Ahram, Al-Akhbar*, and *Al-Gumhuriya*, and their many associated titles) were referred to as the 'national press' (*al-sahafa al-qawmiya*), connoting a duty of patriotism. This connected to a deep sense, shared by government and public, that any portrayal of Egypt or Egyptian affairs should be 'positive': that there could be no tarnishing of the nation's 'image' or 'reputation'.¹⁴ By 2007, after a quarter of a century under Mubarak, government spokesmen were routinely conflating the nation's reputation with Mubarak's. When Ibrahim Eissa, then editor of the independent *El-Destour*, was tried that September after writing a column about the President's health, the ruling party's lawyer accused him of 'inciting people against one of the pillars of the state'.¹⁵

On the other side, since the governments of Nasser and Sadat had changed only when the president died, the party-political newspapers launched under Sadat came to be characterised *de facto* as the 'opposition press' (*al-sahafa al-mu'ardha*). Even though the first incarnation of *El-Destour*, launched as a Cyprus-registered weekly in 1995, was backed neither by government nor a political party, its independent coverage was immediately seen to place it in the 'opposition' camp and the government forced it to cease distribution in 1998. Despite *El-Destour*'s eventual comeback with a local licence in 2004, and the emergence of other independent papers, assumptions about a link between non-government titles and opposition politics stuck. It continues to influence the way some journalists feel they are perceived.

'As an independent journalist you're cornered. You're classified as anti-regime right away, no matter how objective you are', was how one independent journalist expressed her predicament to the writer Maurice Chammah in 2011.¹⁶ Another explained it as follows:

> *When your independence entails bringing out the truth, and the truth is very, very ugly, and it's always against the current regime and the status quo, then you're instantly opposition. So you're always put in this position, unwillingly maybe, and sometimes unintentionally, of opposing the regime, when in fact what you're doing is a completely objective portrayal of certain situations.*[17]

The implication that objective reporting is a form of anti-government activism presents a challenge to all Egyptian journalists, but it is a challenge that is more or less relished depending on the experience and horizons of the journalist concerned. The range of experience is considerable, not only because of Egypt's own different categories of media outlet, but also because of job openings in Arabic-language or Middle East-oriented radio stations in Europe and the USA, as well as the pan-Arab media, which expanded dramatically during the 1990s and early 2000s. Journalists struggling against authoritarianism in other parts of the world have maybe had four options. Colin Sparks, writing about Latin America, summarised them as: accepting censorship for ideological reasons; tolerating it in order to hold down a job; defying the censors even at the risk of paying a heavy price; or 'staying in employment with a collaborationist newspaper or broadcaster while moonlighting for a more radical and oppositional outlet'.[18] All four apply in Egypt. But Egyptians, benefiting from a shared language with other Arabs and increasing Arab migration away from the Arab world, have had other alternatives as well.

It can be hypothesised that mobility between jobs, which increased in parallel with the proliferation of pan-Arab newspapers and satellite channels, helped to foster journalists' determination to assert their own individual interpretations of professional norms. Gulf-owned networks such as MBC, Rotana, Dubai TV, or Al-Jazeera, being based in countries with small indigenous populations, have traditionally needed to recruit from across the Arab world. Egypt's extensive media industry offers a pool of talent. With network owners' political agendas at least partly reflected in each network's editorial output, and with the agendas of different Gulf owners often at odds, any journalist who lost his or her position at either an Egyptian or a Gulf channel for being too independent-minded could reasonably expect to be hired elsewhere.

It is consequently not surprising that Egyptian journalists working in the different possible situations – in Egypt for the Egyptian media, in Egypt for the pan-Arab media, or in Doha and Dubai for the pan-Arab media – were shown to be so conscious of transnational relationships and competition in the mid-2000s that they generally believed themselves to be part of a single professional community.¹⁹ In the heyday of Al-Jazeera's Arabic-language news channel, Egyptians working under constraints in the national setting looked to their compatriots there for role models and inspiration.²⁰ But everything changes, including the pan-Arab media. As the Egyptian media scene developed after 2004–5, Al-Jazeera's star began to wane. A Nielsen poll conducted for Al-Jazeera among 27,000 viewers in 2009 found that Al-Jazeera was 'practically absent' from Egyptian screens.²¹ The earlier flow of Egyptians to the pan-Arab media was now giving way to a flow in the other direction.

Thus, by 2011–12, the 'new breed' of journalists observed by the author of 'The Death of Deference' in 2007 had become even more diverse. The following sections explore some of this diversity among journalists with and without experience of the media outside Egypt. As the first example involving a veteran practitioner shows, the newness of the so-called 'new breed' of journalists had nothing to do with their chronological age.

Hamdi Kandil

Hamdi Kandil, who was hauled before a court in 2010 for an article he wrote in *Al-Shorouk*, started his career in the 1950s under Mustafa Amin, founder of the daily *Al-Akhbar*. In the next half-century he worked in a range of media outlets in Egypt, Jordan, and Dubai, as well as two international organisations: the Arab States Broadcasting Union and UNESCO. When the ERTU felt compelled in 1999 to attract viewers by offering them something comparable to the argumentative political talkshows on Al-Jazeera, it came up with *Ra'is al-Tahrir* (Editor-in-Chief), presented by Kandil. At the time Kandil claimed that the political leadership had 'no objection to greater freedom' but wanted people 'capable of understanding the delicate balances at stake'.²² Later, in 2001, he recounted that his role had been to 'push' to get 'nearer to the red lines', and that he was happy he had 'encouraged national television to take freer steps'. Kandil added: 'I'd rather work for national television. I'd prefer that a government kicks me out one day than a businessman – and I'll be kicked out one day of course.'²³

In the two years between those two interviews, Egypt's television landscape had undergone a structural change, which turned the choice of being sacked by the government or a businessman into a reality. A government decree in 2000 had opened the way to private Egyptian broadcasting companies on conditional terms. They had to transmit by satellite from the country's so-called media free zone, Media Production City; they had to accept part ownership by the ERTU; and they had to refrain from gathering news. Only two of the companies to take advantage of this small degree of liberalisation in the first half of the 2000s, Dream TV and El-Mehwar, sought to get round the news ban by providing current affairs commentary and analysis instead. Dream's programming was steered by Hala Sarhan, who brought in Kandil (after the ERTU axed *Ra'is al-Tahrir* because of his bitter but highly popular treatment of US policy in Afghanistan and Iraq), along with Ibrahim Eissa and Mohammed Hassanein Heikal, to provide political coverage that would attract viewers in large enough numbers to make the channel commercially viable.

Kandil outlasted Sarhan at Dream. She was forced out in 2003 and he stayed until the spring of 2004. Sana Mansour, a retiree from the ERTU who succeeded Sarhan as Dream's manager, blamed Kandil for his own departure.[24] However, the fact that both Sarhan and Eissa had already been removed, and Heikal's outspoken monologues were known to have landed the channel in trouble with its government-controlled licensing body, indicated that Kandil must also have crossed the 'red lines' that he said he had been pushing towards. For the next four years Kandil gained a loyal following as host of *Qalam Rusas* (Pencil) on Dubai TV. When Dubai TV cancelled the show at the end of 2008 he took it to a Libyan satellite channel, which was swiftly silenced by the Libyan regime. When, in May 2010, he wrote an article for *Al-Shorouk*, dealing with burning issues such as renewal of the emergency law and alleged corruption in the sale of Egyptian gas, Mubarak's foreign minister filed a criminal case against him. Given Kandil's other role as spokesperson for Egypt's National Association for Change, which connected him to Mohammed el-Baradei, a potential presidential candidate for 2011, the lawsuit looked like a calculated threat to both his writing and his activism.

Hala Sarhan

Sarhan's own formation as a journalist before and after her brief spell at Dream TV illustrates the revolving door between Egyptian and pan-Arab outlets, and between print and broadcast media. She started out as an ERTU radio announcer and worked for Voice of America and a Saudi-owned women's magazine while in the USA. Returning to Cairo in the 1980s she set up a magazine, *Kul el-Nas* (Everyone), with her husband, Emad Al-Deeb, who was to become a newspaper magnate with holdings in private radio and film. The two divorced and Sarhan worked as a social affairs talkshow host for ART, a Saudi-owned satellite network with studios in Cairo, before joining Dream for its launch in 2001. Her time at Dream was fairly controversial and, as with Kandil, the precise reasons for her departure were never clear. Was it because she discussed female masturbation on a talkshow? Was she held responsible for Heikal's diatribes? Or was the channel's owner, Ahmad Bahgat, induced to tone down Dream's content because he needed financial support from government-controlled banks?

Whatever the reason, Sarhan moved to Saudi-owned Rotana Cinema, where she ran into more trouble in early 2007 when three guests on her programme, who said they were prostitutes working under police protection, claimed afterwards that Sarhan had paid them to lie. Sarhan, charged with endangering public security and promoting licentiousness, stayed away from Egypt for a few years. She made her comeback in June 2011, this time with the newly launched Rotana Masriya (Rotana-Egypt), presenting a nightly two-hour show called *Nassbook* (People Book). Interviewed at the Rotana Masriya studios, Sarhan insisted that the 2007 legal case reflected the Mubarak government's determination to discredit her exposure of Egypt's harsh social realities.[25] Interpretations at the time were mixed. It was an *Al-Ahram* journalist who appeared on El-Mehwar channel to allege the fakery, and El-Mehwar majored on the scandal for a week. Other journalists, including *Sawt al-Umma* editor Wael Ibrashi, condemned the system rather than Sarhan. Makram Mohammed Ahmad, then Journalists' Syndicate head, said he believed Sarhan had been targeted personally and that people accusing her of defaming Egypt's reputation had exaggerated.[26]

Hafez al-Mirazi

Not all Egyptian journalists leaving jobs in the 2000s did so because they were forced to for appearing to take sides against those in power. Sometimes the reason for a departure was a refusal to take sides. Hafez al-Mirazi, one-time news anchor on state radio's *Sawt al-Arab* (Voice of the Arabs) and freelancer for Voice of America, headed Al-Jazeera's Washington bureau for seven eventful years before he left the channel in early 2007. He apparently warned Al-Jazeera on joining that if it ever became subject to censorship he would leave. At the time he saw it as balanced, hosting a range of voices, including those of US and Israeli officials. 'If the network had any kind of agenda or control', he said approvingly during 2006, 'you wouldn't find so much variety in its staff'.[27] A few months later Mirazi felt there was a political agenda. He explained to the Saudi-owned daily *Al-Hayat* in June 2007 that Al-Jazeera's increasingly Islamist outlook and marginalisation of liberal journalists caused him to quit.[28]

Leaving the USA after 24 years, Mirazi sensed that 'change was coming in Egypt' – that Egyptian channels' new talkshows about domestic affairs, combined with a change in the 'internal political environment' in 2004–5, had got viewers 'glued' to programmes about Egypt rather than the pan-Arab talk typical of transnational channels.[29] He used one of the final episodes of his Al-Jazeera programme *Min Washington* (From Washington) to host a panel that was actually held in Cairo and featured three Egyptian talkshow hosts. They were: Mona Shazli of *Al-Ashera Masa'an* (10pm) on Dream 2, Moataz El-Demerdash of *Tessa'in Daqiqa* (90 Minutes) on El-Mehwar, and Mahmoud Saad, then a co-presenter of *El-Beit Beitak* (Make Yourself at Home), a privately produced programme aired on two state (ERTU) channels. Mirazi introduced the panel by countering the widely held assumption that 'America' is a prime focus of Egyptian television talk. He pointed instead to a new phenomenon of 'public dialogue programmes' dealing with local issues.[30] He would later join one of these programmes himself (see below).

Moataz El-Demerdash

Unintentionally perhaps, the December 2006 episode of *Min Washington* provided a forum for comparing approaches to television journalism and journalists' role in public dialogue. Demerdash, with BBC, Reuters, and Voice of America posts on his CV, as well as a seven-year stay in London while working for Saudi-owned MBC, disagreed with Saad on whether a talkshow host should take sides. Saad spoke admiringly of Hamdi Kandil's frequent criticism of the USA and Israel, citing this as the reason for Kandil's popularity with viewers. Saad said that, as an Egyptian citizen, he was equally critical of the USA. Demerdash intervened to suggest that Saad had confused the print journalism practice of writing opinions and the role of presenter of a 'dialogue programme' on television. Even if he wanted personally to attack something, Demerdash said, it was not the role of a presenter to do so. 'We don't offer this media service to ourselves', he argued, 'but to the public, to millions of viewers'.

This approach may explain why Demerdash eventually left El-Mehwar. Asked in 2010 about the proliferation of talkshows on Egyptian channels, he said the phenomenon could 'help shape a freer media'. But, he warned, 'the talk show should address the people's real problems and should be unbiased and free of any political agendas to have credibility'.[31] Such freedom was not in evidence on El-Mehwar on 1 February 2011, when Sayed Ali and Hanaa El-Semary used their show *48 Sa'a* (48 Hours) to try to discredit protestors in Tahrir Square by hosting a woman – her voice, face, and real name all concealed – who claimed she had been trained by 'Jews' in the USA to cause chaos in Egypt. The local press quickly exposed the interviewee as a fake. Demerdash fell out with El-Mehwar's main owner, businessman Hassan Rateb. In May 2011 he was back on the screen with a new interview programme, *Masr el-Gedida* (New Egypt), for a different private channel, Al-Hayat.

Mahmoud Saad

Mahmoud Saad was one of the ERTU journalists who came out against regime propaganda during the 25 January uprising, distinguishing himself from those regime mouthpieces who only changed their tune after Mubarak fell. Government ministers worked hard to obscure the reasons why Saad quit his show, *Masr El-Naharda* (Egypt Today). According to Saad himself, he had come under heavy pressure to criticise anti-government protestors[32] and to interview the new prime minister, Ahmad Shafik, in place of his own chosen interviewee, opposition politician Osama Ghazali Harb. But ministers put out a different version. Shafik told the public, through another television talkshow, that Saad really left because his salary had been cut. The allegation resonated with viewers, who had learned from the information minister, Anas al-Fiqi, earlier in the month, that Saad's salary was £E 9 million ($1.5 million). Fiqi had mentioned the figure while phoning in to *Masr El-Naharda*.[33] Saad's animosity to Shafik about the affair spilled over in May 2012, when Saad used his slot on the Al-Nahar channel to express outrage at Shafik's success in the first round of the presidential election. On being reminded of Al-Nahar's commitment to objectivity, Saad told viewers that objectivity is elusive and that, ever since entering the media, he had always been keen to speak his mind.[34]

Amr Adeeb

In its final years the Mubarak regime appeared sometimes to think that using the media to highlight social divisions could distract attention from government corruption and neglect. In those cases, despite legal prohibitions on journalism deemed to be socially divisive, journalists expressing divisive opinions did so with impunity. Examples include the culling of pigs belonging to Coptic Christians in Cairo during fears about swine flu in April 2009, or accusations of violence between Algerians and Egyptians in connection with World Cup qualifying football matches in November 2009. The voice of talkshow host Amr Adeeb on the daily *Al-Qahira al-Youm* (Cairo Today) was sometimes dominant on such occasions. A producer on the show recalls that Adeeb was one of the first to draw the connection between swine flu, pigs, and rubbish collection in Egypt, and that the government ordered the cull the next day.[35] Early in the Algeria–Egypt football crisis, Adeeb suggested on air that Algerians harboured an unreasonable hatred for Egypt. 'I would love to see an end to their arrogance', he said.[36] In a later programme, with allegations raging about attacks on Egyptians, Adeeb's co-host, Ahmad Moussa, deputy chief editor of *Al-Ahram*, was interpreted by his own programme team to have incited Egyptians to attack Algerians in the street.[37]

Adeeb's idiosyncratic approach to public talk about news influenced the Egyptian media during a critical period in its evolution, even though his programme aired on a Saudi channel, Orbit, not an Egyptian one. The show started in a magazine-variety format at the very end of 1999, before private Egyptian channels emerged. In 2004 a new information minister instructed the ERTU to commission a copy-cat programme, in the form of *El-Beit Beitak*. From 2005, Adeeb increasingly took the limelight on *Al-Qahira al-Youm* as a political commentator, apparently shielded from repercussions because of his connections to the power elite. But his handling of sensitive political topics was often wayward and, in September 2010, the government silenced him by closing Orbit's Cairo operation on the pretext of payment arrears. Given the high profile of callers to *Al-Qahira al-Youm* and its frequent mentions in the press, observers saw its suspension as the government's way of minimising public probing in the run-up to parliamentary elections in November 2010. Adeeb signed a contract with Al-Hayat to host a new show with a start date of January 2011, after the elections were over.

Tawfik Okasha

It can be surmised that, where opinionated journalism is prevalent, its prevalence influences both audience expectations and aspiring journalists. In such an environment there is a risk that the most extreme forms of media partisanship and fabrication blend in with their surroundings, or elicit comment that merely takes an opposite view without expanding the amount of verified information citizens need to make sound choices. Mubarak and his ruling party, the NDP, used a few supposedly private outlets as proxies to discredit dissidents and human rights activists by accusing them of promoting Western imperialist interference in Egypt's affairs. Al-Fara'een, owned by talkshow host and NDP member Tawfik Okasha, served this role for Mubarak's successors. After the channel urged viewers onto the streets in November 2011 to show their support for SCAF, a leaked document revealed an airforce general's assessment that Al-Fara'een's programmes were 'neutral, objective and put the nation's interests above all considerations'.[38]

Divergent paths

It emerges from the account so far that Egypt may have as many, if not more, prominent journalists keen to speak their own minds as journalists who believe their job is to let sources or facts speak for themselves. Such a situation would not be surprising. Decades of obstacles to obtaining or publishing accurate information about the workings of government or the state of society favoured the filling of column inches with opinion. The ease with which prominent media practitioners crossed between print and broadcast outlets, as the latter expanded, no doubt favoured the import of editorialising into television. The ban on privately owned television channels making their own newscasts during the Mubarak era was a further factor to thwart organic development of broadcast news reporting. Added to these were legal strictures, contained in the press law, penal code, and a July 2008 bill on regulation of audio-visual media, against any treatment, by news or commentary, of topics deemed to be damaging to 'social peace', 'national unity', or 'public values'. The high profile of some opinionated media practitioners exemplifies how public and professional confusion over the purpose of journalism and over understandings of journalistic ethics could be exploited for political ends.

Such an environment forces journalists who do strive for objectivity to struggle on multiple fronts. The next section dissects some actual struggles and the precedents they set for journalism that distinguishes between reporting and opinion.

Individuals vs institutions

Prominent private investors with diverse interests in business and industry played a leading role in creating new outlets in Egypt's partly liberalised media sector from 2001. But while opening up space for successful journalism, these owners added another layer of complexity to a media system already stacked against professional autonomy and objective reporting in various hidden ways. The evidence shows that ownership issues, problematic before January 2011 because of business links to the Mubarak regime, remained equally so after it. But it also shows that variations in ownership arrangements among outlets have the potential to produce diverse outcomes in terms of journalism. Owners can be alert to the financial implications of firing or retaining a journalist who is trusted by the public and has gained a loyal following.

Hisham Kassem

Hisham Kassem, himself more publisher than journalist, grappled with some of the hidden systemic complexities during the lifetime of his ground-breaking English-language paper, *Cairo Times* (1997–2004), and his period managing *Al-Masry al-Youm*, from before its launch in 2004 to his resignation in 2008. Accounts of his trials of strength with state censors are legendary: when *Cairo Times* joined only two other Egyptian papers to report on police brutality in the mainly Christian village of Al-Kosheh in 1998, the state authorities went from criminalising mere possession of a copy of that issue to realising that the *Cairo Times* report, written from local knowledge and perspectives, was more accurate and less damaging than versions circulating in the international press.[39] *Cairo Times* made strategic use of its website to publish stories that the authorities insisted on cutting from the print edition, and forged alliances with printers and distributors to sustain its presence in the market. At the same time Kassem learned other lessons, which he applied in his dealings with the owners, editors, and advertising sales team of *Al-Masry al-Youm*.

The lessons relate to things like salaries and employment practices, relations with security officials and advertisers, and gaining a reputation for reliability. Although a few staff in the state media commanded very high salaries under Mubarak, and some television celebrities in private channels have been able to do likewise, journalists' salaries are generally very low, as is the case for many occupations in Egypt. With no official state safety net, and massive overstaffing in the public sector, an unofficial safety net has developed whereby employees may take on two or more jobs and show limited commitment to any. This state of affairs leaves journalists vulnerable to external financial inducements. Kassem's approach in *Al-Masry al-Youm* was to recruit young graduates, offer competitive salaries, one-year renewable contracts with performance-based pay increases, and to instruct staff to refer any contact from state authorities directly to him. He is known to have fought with editors and advertising staff to keep a strict dividing line between editorial and advertising, and insisted on publishing corrections.

Kassem's objective, as summarised when he received a National Endowment for Democracy award in Washington in September 2007, was to establish a 'newspaper of record with objective reporting and transparency in its ownership'. The businessmen investing in *Al-Masry al-Youm* were led by Salah Diab, who made his fortune with Egypt's first oil services company, together with telecom magnate Nagib Sawiris and Ahmad Bahgat, owner of a consumer electronics and real estate empire as well as Dream TV. Sawiris, whose previous media investments were in music and entertainment, expanded into factual television when he launched ONTV in October 2008. ONTV's management said they chose the channel's motto, 'Stay in the Light', to convey liberal values of 'citizenship, freedom, equality, modernization [and] rationality'.[40]

Sawiris and his co-investors mostly backed Kassem in his internal confrontations with *Al-Masry al-Youm* staff and were rewarded with an apparently profitable and respected newspaper. Readership increased spectacularly after the paper investigated election fraud in November 2005 and the media environment was structurally altered by expansion in the number of newspapers that were neither government-controlled, nor specifically anti-government. The next business venture to fit the category was *Al-Shorouk*, in 2007, followed by *Al-Youm al-Sabea* in 2008. But Kassem eventually had reasons for leaving *Al-Masry al-Youm*. He objected to a rearrangement of ownership shares[41] and wanted to start work on a new project for a converged multimedia newsroom, which would carry out investigative journalism. The economic downturn caused by political instability in 2011 affected the investors behind Kassem's multimedia project and delayed its start.

Ibrahim Eissa

For *Al-Masry al-Youm* the political will and financial resilience of its multiple owners were crucial to the kind of journalism it could engage in. The same turned out to be true, in reverse, when the scathingly anti-corruption newspaper *El-Destour* changed hands in 2010 and its trademark character was, in the words of *Al-Ahram Weekly*, 'diluted to the point of extinction' as a result.[42] Founded by Essam Ismail Fahmy in the 1990s and silenced by the government for six years, *El-Destour* did well enough after its return to the news-stands in 2004 to switch from a weekly to a daily, complete with website. In August 2010, at a moment when the NDP was doing all it could to ensure a crushing victory in the coming parliamentary elections, Fahmy sold the paper for a reported £E 20 million[43] ($3.3 million) to two businessmen at the helm of the opposition Wafd Party, namely El-Sayed El-Badawy of Sigma Pharmaceuticals and Al-Hayat TV, and Reda Edward, owner of a chain of private schools. Fahmy said the new shareholders believed in *El-Destour*'s role in 'defending freedoms, promoting reform and democracy'.[44]

Weeks later, *El-Destour*'s renowned dissident editor-in-chief, Ibrahim Eissa, and his executive editor, Ibrahim Mansour, were sacked. Eissa's colleagues, who went on strike in protest at the sacking, attributed it to an article that Eissa insisted on running by Mohammed el-Baradei, aspiring 2011 presidential candidate. In the article, which eventually appeared in print and on the website, Baradei listed 'values essential to the advancement of societies', which, he wrote, were missing in Egyptian society. They included 'citizenship, team work, logical thinking, planning, punctuality, loyalty, honesty, modesty, transparency and self-denial'. However, the departure of Eissa and Mansour also seemed to have more fundamental causes. It appeared to prove that the Wafd Party, far from being a real opposition party, was helping the NDP to silence its critics. After Eissa's supporters advocated a boycott of Sigma Pharmaceuticals, Badawy sold his share in *El-Destour* to Edward and left him in charge.

This was not Badawy's first change of heart about a media venture under pressure from the regime. He had planned to launch Al-Hayat TV in January 2008 with Hafez al-Mirazi as co-founder, running a large-scale nationwide news-gathering operation with 40 reporters in 30 Egyptian towns and cities. By stationing correspondents around the country, Al-Hayat would pre-empt the difficulties all the media faced from state security when trying to send someone from Cairo into an outlying area. As far as Mirazi knew, Badawy had been reliably informed that the operation would be permitted provided it left Mubarak and his family alone and refrained from giving a platform to Islamists.[45] But the government apparently sensed that more was planned for the regional reporters than merely covering local municipal news. The information minister, Anas el-Fiqi, tried to tempt Mirazi to drop Al-Hayat by offering him the directorship of Nile News, which Mirazi refused. A week later, Badawy let Mirazi know that the news-gathering project was off, that Al-Hayat would focus on entertainment, and that Mirazi's role would not exceed hosting one show that should focus on the USA.[46] Mirazi parted company with Al-Hayat and in 2008 took over as director of the Adham Center for Television and Digital Journalism at the American University in Cairo.

Ibrahim Eissa, having had an equally unsatisfactory relationship with El-Sayed El-Badawy in 2010, was also elbowed out of his place as co-host of *Baladna bil-Masry* on ONTV during the same pre-election purge of 2010 that had removed Amr Adeeb and others. By leaving ONTV at that point he helped to reduce government pressure on Nagib Sawiris. Sawiris, whose family belonged to a network of elite businesses that benefited from close contacts with government over several decades, admitted immediately after Mubarak's removal: 'Even someone like me was scared [of the regime].' He told Charlie Rose of PBS on 14 February 2011 that he had asked an assistant to gather all the interviews he had done in Egypt on a CD, just for his own purposes, to check all the phrases that he was 'risking saying': 'Because if you went a little bit overboard the next day something will be faked against you or your interests will be hit.'[47]

Sawiris, Badawy, and Edward were not alone in avoiding risks with the Mubarak regime. El-Mehwar's owner, Hassan Rateb, confirmed to *Al-Masry al-Youm* that he always obtained state security clearance before hiring anyone, while Dream TV's owner, Ahmad Bahgat, speaking to the same paper in the summer of 2010, said he would 'shut Dream down' if the government requested it. 'What else could we do?', he asked. 'Would we challenge the state?'[48] With Mubarak's departure, many hoped this level of government leverage on media investors would reduce. Disappointment was to come, however, as illustrated by several incidents in 2011 and 2012, the most revealing of which were those involving television journalists Dina Abdel-Rahman, Hafez al-Mirazi, and Yosri Fouda. The experiences of these three shed light on the relative strengths of journalists and owners in the face of a ruling military power that perpetuated many elements of the previous regime.

Dina Abdel-Rahman

Dina Abdel-Rahman, presenter of a morning show on Dream, was sacked twice, once by Bahgat and the second time by Suleiman Amer, after he became the new owner of Tahrir TV. Both incidents attracted attention in other media, online and offline, which gave Abdel-Rahman and her production team a platform from which to recount their own versions of what happened, and set precedents for other journalists seeking to assert values of professionalism and autonomy. Abdel-Rahman hosted *Sabah Dream* (Dream Morning) for five years until, on 24 July 2011, she was called into Bahgat's office ten minutes after her show and told that another presenter would replace her with immediate effect. That morning's show had been notable for an exchange between Abdel-Rahman and retired General Abdel-Moneim Kato, adviser to the armed forces, who telephoned in to the programme to complain that Abdel-Rahman had mentioned an article in *Al-Tahrir* newspaper by Naglaa Bedeir. Kato labelled Bedeir a subversive and accused her of defaming his colleague, Major General Hassan el-Rowainy.

Bedeir's point in the article, based on Rowainy's own lengthy and controversial comments on a previous episode of *Sabah Dream*,[49] had been that Rowainy was resorting to the failed rhetoric of the Mubarak regime, which included smearing any opponent as having a foreign agenda or suspicious ties. Abdel-Rahman defended Bedeir's professionalism and integrity, but Kato adopted Rowainy's logic. He accused two unnamed presidential candidates and the April 6 movement of having suspicious ties with the USA and declared that the armed forces were now trying to teach the Egyptian people 'basic democracy'.[50]

Sabah Dream's producer, Jihane Aboul-Ella, was furious that Abdel-Rahman should be let go for this incident and shared her feelings with reporters. Yosri Fouda, host of ONTV's *Akher Kalam* (Last Word), immediately tweeted in solidarity, and several social media sites set up pages to support Abdel-Rahman and advocate a boycott of goods from Bahgat's factories. Bahgat did not relent. The exchange with Kato was omitted from the rerun of that episode and an attempt at mediation by another Dream presenter, Ahmad al-Mislimani, widely respected for his media and politics show *Tabaa Oula* (First Edition), did not succeed. Soon afterwards, Abdel-Rahman and her team signed up with Tahrir TV to present a late-night show called *Al-Youm* (The Day). According to Abdel-Rahman, she chose Tahrir TV after declining an offer from ONTV, because the ONTV offer would have made her beholden to Nagib Sawiris. Even though Bahgat had effectively dismissed Abdel-Rahman, his company insisted that the £E 1 million ($165,000) penalty for breaking her contract was still payable; Sawiris, tied to both Dream and ONTV through his advertising sales company Promomedia, offered to pay it.[51]

Abdel-Rahman said Tahrir TV suited her for two reasons. First, it was not controlled by tycoons or 'influential people'; and secondly, its founders had a vision of television content that was 'unbiased' and 'professional', 'in harmony with my own principles'.[52] In the autumn of 2011, observers took the move as a signal that Tahrir TV would stick to this vision despite Ibrahim Eissa having sold his share. But *Al-Youm* only lasted on Tahrir TV until February 2012. It was cancelled after a further ownership change, when the new management wanted to revise Abdel-Rahman's contract to deny her autonomy in choosing topics or guests for *Al-Youm* and to prevent her taking any legal dispute with the channel to court. The new owner, Suleiman Amer, had personal experience of Abdel-Rahman's commitment to balance. She had once insisted, during a 2008 episode of *Sabah Dream*, that if Amer came on the show to defend his property developments on Egypt's scarce agricultural land, he should be challenged by someone from the Ministry of Agriculture. After the dispute over her contract with Tahrir TV, Amer's staff leaked copies of it to the press, showing her salary, ID number, and home address.[53]

Hafez al-Mirazi

Hafez al-Mirazi is another journalist to have made a stand for autonomy inside more than one media operation in post-Mubarak Egypt. His earlier stand at Al-Hayat has already been noted in the discussion of Ibrahim Eissa's relationship with Al-Hayat's owner, El-Sayed El-Badawy. So has his reason for leaving Al-Jazeera. In February 2011, the day after Mubarak's removal, Mirazi stood up for his editorial rights in the Saudi-owned news channel Al-Arabiya, where he hosted a daily talkshow called *Studio Al-Qahira* (Cairo Studio). He announced at the end of that night's show that he intended the next day to discuss the implications of the Egyptian revolution for Saudi Arabia. The next day came, and the next, and there was no *Studio Al-Qahira*. Instead, ten days later, Mirazi appeared on Dream 2's *Al-Ashera Masa'an* explaining, much to host Mona Shazli's amusement, that Al-Arabiya had initially reacted by making *Studio Al-Qahira* weekly, to give Mirazi time to change his mind, and when he refused, they decided to make it monthly or 'maybe even an annual show'.[54]

In the following months, as Essam Sharaf's government turned its attention to state-owned television, it nominated Mirazi as one of 13 public figures on the ERTU Board of Trustees. By then he had also been lined up to host a talkshow on an ERTU channel, with the title *Bi Tawqit el-Qahira* (By Cairo Time) – a pointed reference to the pan-Arab channels' practice of announcing programme schedules by reference to Mecca time. Worried about a conflict of interests, Mirazi says he wrote to Sharaf, asking him either to freeze his status on the board, or to accept his resignation. Tarik al-Mahdi, the airforce general drafted in to oversee the ERTU and an *ex-officio* board member, saw no problem with Mirazi playing both roles. So Mirazi resigned, pointing out in his resignation letter the anomaly of having a military man in a two-year appointment to the Board of Trustees of a civilian institution when military rule over Egypt was due to last no longer than one year.[55] *Bi Tawqit el-Qahira* failed to air as promised in early June and Mirazi took the show instead to Dream 2.

What happened next is attributable at least in part to Bahgat's cross-ownership of two leading media outlets: Dream TV and *Al-Masry al-Youm*. Interviewing *Al-Masry al-Youm* editor Magdi Galad in an episode of *Bi Tawqit el-Qahira*, Mirazi confronted Galad unexpectedly with a YouTube clip showing Galad expressing support for Gamal Mubarak as a potential future president. When Dream reran several episodes of *Bi Tawqit el-Qahira* during Mirazi's absence in the USA over the 2012 New Year holiday, Mirazi learned that Dream TV's CEO, Osama Ezzeddin, was planning to doctor the episode containing the uncomfortable exchange with Galad. Bahgat was apparently worried about the impact on Galad's prestige. Mirazi objected to the deletion on two grounds. First, it contravened his contract, which made him responsible for decisions about content in his programme. Secondly, it risked normalising double standards on the part of journalists, like Galad, who like to challenge others without being challenged themselves.[56] After suspending his contract, and making sure his reasons were publicly known, Mirazi eventually resumed his show on Dream.

Yosri Fouda

Yosri Fouda also conducted his struggle – to keep control over his choice of guests and topics on *Akher Kalam* – in public. Fouda's formation as a journalist included an assignment in Bosnia in the mid-1990s, when he worked with the BBC during its first shortlived experiment with Arabic-language television, after which he became part of Al-Jazeera's original team and presenter of its programme *Sirri l'il-Ghaya* (Top Secret). As co-author of a book called *Masterminds of Terror*, based on interviews with some very dangerous men in inhospitable places, Fouda accepts another writer's description of him as an 'Egyptian sleuth' who 'almost single-handedly pioneered the Arab tradition of investigative journalism'.[57] Fouda was two years into his contract with ONTV when, on 21 October 2011, he suspended his show in protest at what happened to it the night before.

Fouda had been due to host Alaa al-Aswany and Ibrahim Eissa to talk about the killing of Libya's former leader Muammar Qaddafi, and analyse an interview that two generals representing SCAF had just given jointly to Tahrir TV and Dream. The episode of *Akher Kalam*, after being announced, did not take place. Fouda issued a statement to say there had been an intervention to prevent the panel going ahead as planned. In the statement, Fouda blamed those in power who believe that 'the media can deny existing realities or create realities that do not exist'. He said he had taken a stand as a journalist to testify to the 'marked deterioration in freedom of professional media' and a complacent acceptance of 'cheap and propaganda-style journalism'.[58]

Returning to his presenter's chair again on 13 November, with the same guests he had planned to host three weeks earlier, Fouda said his stand had achieved its aim. 'Someone has to draw a line somewhere', he later told the BBC. 'I'm not going to wait until they come to my studio with machine guns.'[59] Part of his leverage in trying to draw a line, at least vis-à-vis ONTV, was evident in the extended advertisement breaks on the 13 November show. According to ONTV director Albert Shafik in January 2012, *Akher Kalam*'s success in attracting advertisements and hits to the website was good for the channel as a whole.[60]

Thus practitioners committed to drawing a line between professional and unprofessional journalism had to accept more or less permanent uncertainty as to their place of employment after January 2011. But trusted journalists could also pull levers to demonstrate the level of their public support. After indicating to close associates that he planned to end his current arrangement with ONTV on 30 June 2012, Fouda duly announced in mid-May that he would quit in six weeks' time.[61] On 21 June, shortly before his self-imposed deadline, Fouda notified followers via Twitter that he had stopped his show for a second time, since Tuesday, out of 'respect' for viewers. ONTV's explanation was that Fouda was exhausted. But Essam Sultan, deputy head of the Wasat Party and a member of the Parliament that was dissolved on 29 June, told reporters that Fouda took his decision because Sultan had been prevented from going on air.[62] Sultan had lodged a complaint with a Cairo Court at the end of May, alleging corruption on the part of presidential candidate Ahmad Shafik for selling land cheaply to the sons of Hosni Mubarak. Shafik left Egypt for the UAE almost immediately after losing the election. Referring to Fouda, Sultan said 'he and those like him are bright candles in a media that is full of fear, humiliation and business'.[63]

Fouda's message on Twitter and Sultan's statement on Facebook demonstrated that any battle of wills between journalists, media owners, and the military over the right to decide editorial content would quickly become public knowledge, no matter who wanted it hidden. The incident also hinted that ONTV's management might not always be strong enough, or inclined, to face down the government on its journalists' behalf, despite its owner's personal wealth, international stature, and foreign business holdings. Given the evidence listed here of several other mainstream offline outlets succumbing to political pressure for self-censorship, the question must be asked as to the possibilities for battling on behalf of professional journalism in a different arena, where financial strength is possibly less critical, namely online.

Attitudes to social media as tools of news-gathering

Cairo Times's use of the internet in 2000 to publish material censored from the newspaper's print edition shows that Egyptian journalists have been asserting their autonomy online for a long time. The harsher censorship became, the more political content – including reporting – was driven onto the internet. Often, as noted in the introduction to this chapter, it emerged in the blogosphere, to the point where the preponderance of political blogs in Egypt influenced perceptions of blogging across the Arab world. Egyptian blogs proliferated in line with developments surrounding the launch of the Kefaya (Enough) opposition movement in 2004 and two sets of elections (presidential and parliamentary) in 2005. According to an estimate by a technical unit attached to the Egyptian cabinet, the number of blogs rose from 40 in 2004 to some 160,000 four years later. Of these, fewer than 10 per cent were written exclusively in English. Over 50 per cent of bloggers were aged between 20 and 30 and more than 25 per cent were women.[64]

Some of Egypt's best known political bloggers gained experience as journalists in formal media institutions. Hossam el-Hamalawy covered protests and repression for *Cairo Times* in 2002 before becoming Cairo correspondent for the *Los Angeles Times*. He contributed to Bloomberg News and the BBC and held senior or founding positions with *Al-Badeel*, *Egypt Independent*, and *AhramOnline*. Nawara Negm trained on the magazine *Al-Shabab* (Youth) in the 1990s and then worked at *Al-Ahram Weekly* and the women's magazine *Nisf al-Dunya* (Half the World). Wael Abbas, renowned for his video testimony of police brutality, worked as a journalist and photographer for *El-Destour* and as Middle East correspondent for the German news agency, DPA. *Al-Ahram*'s deputy business editor, Sabah Hammamou, posted a video blog of police brutality on YouTube at the start of the protests in January 2011. Bloggers like these took the lead in acting as watchdogs of state corruption, demonstrating how individual news workers can deploy digital media to compensate for failures of offline media systems.

Facebook was put to similar use. It took off in Egypt in January 2008 when users found it a good way to support their national football team in the Africa Cup, and was quickly deployed by the April 6 Youth Movement as a mobilising tool for strikes and protests. But Facebook also offered a means of expression for individuals. AUC professor Rasha Abdallah said at the time: 'We are a repressed country ... people jump at any opportunity to speak their mind.'[65] At the same time Facebook allowed alternative media such as internet radio station Horytna, launched in 2007, to connect with listeners and, in 2010, was the original operating medium for Rassd News Network. With 11.3 million Facebook users by mid-2012, Egypt had the 19th largest number in the world. This was equivalent to just over 14 per cent of the country's total population but over 66 per cent of its internet users.[66]

Twitter use spread quickly in 2008–9, for similar reasons to Facebook. Conventional wisdom states that Twitter was picked up regionally after its effectiveness was demonstrated during June 2009 protests over the presidential election in Iran. Closer scrutiny shows that Egyptian activists used it during the April 2008 protests. Nora Younis, who tweeted news about 6 April strikes and detainees, said her followers on Twitter increased from 90 on 5 April to 130 on 6 April, and 180 by the end of the month.[67] Younis had been working as a fixer for a crew from PBS in the USA when she started blogging in 2005. She later contributed coverage to the *Washington Post* and in August 2008 she joined *Al-Masry al-Youm*, heading its multimedia desk and overseeing pages on citizen journalism.

Wael Abbas relied on Twitter during April 2009 to alert his contacts when he was detained and interrogated for allegedly assaulting a police officer.[68] By March 2011, with the number of known active users in Egypt having exceeded 131,200,[69] the micro-blogging tool provided a platform for breaking news. Local journalist Rasha Azab tweeted her testimony on 9 March when military police forced virginity tests on protestors in their custody. News of the abuse was picked up in the foreign media, but took another two months to make an impact in the Egyptian press. 25TV, which launched in April 2011, introduced a programme called *Hashtag*, entirely devoted to activity in the twittersphere. After the events in Tahrir Square, television talkshows were keen to hire bloggers and online activists with an understanding of social media, who could alert other staff to news leads. Shahira Amin, who walked out of the ERTU in February 2011 and later returned to Nile TV as presenter of a weekly show recorded outside the ERTU building, was part of this trend. She told an interviewer: 'I do incorporate a lot of the things I find on social media in my work ... Sometimes I say, if it has not been tweeted, then it is not newsworthy.'[70]

Take-up of blogging and social media in Egypt amply demonstrated how participatory, cross-media journalism could act as a corrective to the shortcomings of offline news media not only in reporting events, but also in doing so with a fuller range of voices and perspectives. Yet Egyptians differ as to whether the potential for alliances between online journalism and activism serves or undermines the cause of those professional journalists who strive for objectivity and balance. As this book has shown, journalists within the better-resourced media institutions have an uphill battle to establish fair reporting and internal pluralism as a norm. In 2009 that concern was behind a plea by Yosri Fouda and Lawrence Pintak (Mirazi's predecessor at the AUC's Adham Center) for differentiation between journalists and activist bloggers in the interests of placing value on reporting 'fact', not 'rumour or innuendo'.[71]

Fouda and Pintak, writing on the website of *Columbia Journalism Review*, called on defenders of press freedom, such as Reporters sans

Frontières and the Committee to Protect Journalists, to concentrate on defending journalists, leaving Amnesty International and other human rights bodies to defend activists who are also bloggers. They suggested that to treat both as journalists was to undermine 'efforts to bolster a free and professional media in the Arab world and Iran'. The authors acknowledged that postings by bloggers such as Wael Abbas had helped to create 'safe space' for journalists to cover previously taboo stories and to 'goad' them into doing so. But they called for clear differentiation between professional journalists and those writers who 'spout vitriol' or 'flog a cause'.[72]

To some extent the plea seemed to demonstrate a common set of reactions among professional journalists everywhere to the converged media environment. Indiana University journalism professor Mark Deuze had identified these in 2008 as: defensiveness; nostalgia for the traditional understanding of what it meant to be a journalist before convergence; and a fear of professional autonomy being undermined through a shift to other sources. For Deuze such reactions were unsurprising, given that professional journalism's 'essential role' in providing society with 'some form of social cement' was being undermined by media managers keen to exploit convergence as a reason to 'depopulate' the profession, and by audiences who like to bypass journalists.[73] For Fouda, however, his appeal was by no means a case of nostalgia for tradition. On the contrary, it reflected his awareness, based on experience, that basic rules of journalism such as checking facts and being transparent about sources had yet to be established across the Egyptian media scene.

Speaking at the start of 2012, as newly elected MPs took their seats in the first post-Mubarak Parliament, Fouda intimated that it was sometimes harder to be a journalist in post-revolution Egypt than in a war zone. He cited an occasion when former NDP secretary general Hossam Badrawy appeared on *Akher Kalam*. Fouda had thought it important for someone who had been with Mubarak during the latter's last 48 hours in office to share their recollections with viewers. But so many of Fouda's friends and colleagues objected so strongly to an NDP official receiving any airtime at all that he felt obliged to step momentarily outside the role of professional practitioner and remind them personally about the tenets of professional journalism.[74] 'That's what my programme is for', he said on another occasion, 'to give the other narrrative':

> Once you accept self-censorship you start to lose things inside your conscience. If I knew there is another narrative I [would] have to make

it known ... I am very much aware of the difference between journalism and activism and I never crossed that line. I am now defending my very profession.[75]

Other voices, however, argued strongly in favour of activist citizen journalism, such as that achieved through the supply of cameras to mothers of civilian detainees undergoing military trials to enable them to film court proceedings. From the activist point of view, the mainstream media only rely on citizen journalist footage to hide their failure to assign a reporter to get pictures of their own. They benefit from footage obtained by unpaid individuals, sometimes at great risk, but provide nothing in return. For activists, the only advantage of this one-sided relationship is to shame the mainstream media into pushing at censorship boundaries. 'We don't have to pretend we're neutral because the world is not neutral. We chose a side', Lubna Darwish of the Mosireen media collective said in March 2012. But while accepting that Mosireen footage is 'part of the propaganda of the revolution', Darwish also insists on its credibility, asserting that every source is vetted and every item checked.[76]

Some might also argue that young Egyptians using social media in the months before Mubarak's overthrow were more likely than not to learn the expectations of fairness and openness to other opinions that are usually associated with professional, objective journalism. A researcher who worked with university students from diverse social class backgrounds in Alexandria and Cairo in late 2010 found users of Facebook to be 'politically savvy, bold, creative, outward looking, group regulating, and ethical'.[77] Users were enjoined not to use the Facebook space to 'insult each other's religion, for pornography or sexual harassment, for advertising or selling things, for spreading false rumours, or for spying'. If the codes were broken, others would intervene by posting a corrective comment, discussing the breach online, or 'de-friending' the offender.[78]

A similar ethic could be seen in the *Tweet Nadwa* (Tweet Seminar) gatherings of bloggers and activists, convened by blogger Alaa Abdel-Fattah and others in Cairo in 2011. Connecting people on the ground and in cyberspace, the gatherings shared tips and principles. Points raised in the August *nadwa* included the desirability of multiple sources covering the same event, and the benefits of avoiding a political agenda, so as to shed light on citizens and their problems without any specific political goal.[79] Asked in 2012 whether they regarded Twitter as a 'closed realm', some of Egypt's best known Twitter users spoke of it in terms that might equally apply to any other news medium: 'There are journalists on Twitter who regard it as a news source'; 'it is a reflection of society'; 'Twitter reflects whatever topics are being discussed at any moment'; 'it's where you find people who share similar views'; 'it's a consultation and consensus-building platform'; 'the default publicness of conversations can lead to interesting results'.[80]

In the Egyptian media market, the low cost of gathering and circulating news through online platforms has an ethical dimension in its own right, because of its link to the 'public interest' element of journalistic professionalism. Audiences for offline newspapers and television channels are suspicious of the high salaries they pay to prominent people and assume these are tied to an editorial agenda. Mohammed Gohar, who gave his channel 25TV a budget of £E 3 million (around $0.5 million) for its first year, calculated that he could manage without the 'insanely high wages' that other TV stations pay their 'so-called media super stars' and the 'fancy décors in the studios that cost hundreds of thousands'. He said 25TV would save money by filming outdoors.[81] Like 25TV, Core Publications runs its youth-oriented magazines with a staff aged mostly under 30. In 2012, having long ago dropped the idea of spending money to transmit a satellite television channel, Core's founder, Shady Sherif, started an internet TV station, El-Gomhoreya, starring personalities still aspiring to celebrity status.

By trying to share the credibility and independence that social media and low-cost digital sites are assumed to enjoy, commercial news enterprises make a virtue out of blurring the distinction between media users and producers. Gohar, who had 28 bloggers among 25TV's reporters in mid-2012, framed the process in terms of pre-empting a threat to the traditional broadcast industry. Social media reach their audience much faster than traditional media, he told the Egyptian magazine *Business Today*: 'You have very expensive writers sitting in air-conditioned offices and writing fantastic scripts while anyone walking around with a phone in his pocket is a journalist himself.' That 'guy with a phone' was once considered a client, but 'now these lines are not there anymore'.[82]

This could be judged, in line with Deuze's diagnosis, as a case of media investors exploiting convergence to minimise outlay on journalistic staff.[83] Or it may qualify as an example of a professional media organisation deliberately tapping into 'the emerging participatory media online in order to produce some kind of co-creative commons-based news platform'.[84] 25TV's profits and whether they are reinvested will decide.

In the meantime, in a labour market rife with distortions and chronic unemployment, it may not be completely fair to distinguish between aspiring journalists according to whether or not they are paid. One-quarter of Egypt's population is aged 18–29 and the jobless rate in that age group is around 60 per cent.[85]

Ultimately, the place of social media in Egyptian journalism has also to be assessed in relation to restrictions imposed by state security agencies. Even though Egypt's intelligence apparatus makes allowance for the fact that the internet reaches less than a third of the population, it still interferes in online news content, especially anything touching on military affairs. Activists know from experience that the security forces use Facebook for monitoring and spreading misinformation. Yet the same activists also believe that social media offer the only means to spread information 'without the editorial interference of newspapers' managements and the state', for reasons of fluidity and speed as well as subject matter.[86]

Journalists in newspaper websites share this judgement. News workers in the online version of *Al-Masry al-Youm* pass news leads from social media sites to the newspaper's reporters. But if they have news items deemed too sensitive for publication offline, the managing editor says he puts them online just long enough for social media users to pick them up and put them into circulation.[87] Thus news leads and first-hand reporting take priority over balance and multiple perspectives in an environment where powerful figures in government and the military have a vested interest in repression and secrecy. The standards that unpaid bloggers and social media users set for themselves may not be occupational standards in the same way as those of paid journalists in the mainstream media, but the evidence suggests there are ethical standards and standards of credibility and they are shared.

As for multiple perspectives, some professionals in offline media believe that current levels of pluralism across the range of media outlets compensate for a lack of pluralism inside them. Amr al-Khafagy, editor-in-chief of *Al-Shorouk*, made this point to the Arab Media Forum in Dubai in May 2012. Khafagy, who also presents ONTV's *Massa' El-Sabt* (Saturday Evening) show and originated the *Al-Ashera Masa'an* format on Dream 2, said that media users are smart enough to handle the fact that the 'same piece of news is commented upon and presented in different ways'. They know that 'all news organisations have affiliations and sport their own agenda', he said, 'so a news organisation having an agenda does not automatically detract from the credibility of its reporting'.[88]

Others working in 'big' media are more cautious, given the critical phase that Egypt is going through. ONTV's Albert Shafik says he is constantly aware that his station 'can take a small event and make it massive, simply because we're broadcasting it into millions of homes'. Thus, in his view, a mass medium must apply 'an element of self-restraint'. 'There are a lot of political problems, a lot of religious factions and grievances between the social classes in Egypt', Shafik told an interviewer in 2011. 'So we have to think carefully about how we're going to tackle each of those issues if we want to truly benefit the country.'[89] Journalists' ideas about the desirability and practicability of creating an internally pluralist media in the public interest are examined in the next chapter.

3

Stimuli for a Public Service Ethos

> Public service media are only one element in a democratically diverse media landscape, alongside private commercial media, party political media, minority media, community media, and so on. Although some of these are present and highly vocal, Egypt's landscape is dominated by state-run publishing and broadcasting entities with a combined workforce of some 74,000 and debts estimated at $3.5 billion. Journalists have led the call for transformation of state-run operations into public service media, but doubts remain about the wider vision for financing and regulating Egyptian news media as a whole.

With the chant *Al-shaab yurid isqat al-nizam* (The people want to topple the regime), protestors in Tahrir Square reclaimed agency for the Egyptian public. For decades the idea of 'the people' had been hijacked by dictators, through the rigging of elections to the People's Assembly, local councils, and trade unions, and the imposition of appointment in place of election in many other bodies.[1] Extensive denial of political participation and representation, compounded by government control over large parts of the media and over any attempt to conduct polls or surveys,[2] effectively voided the term 'public opinion' of weight in the Egyptian context. In its place came the phrase 'Arab street', which not only obscured the diversity and openness of public opinion in Egypt and the Arab world but, in constructing such opinion as 'volatile and irrational', impeded engagement with it.[3]

In any society, the potential for public opinion to be articulated comprehensively and accurately is bound up with the system of media ownership and regulation. Proponents of public service media see such media as a core element in a pluralistic democratic system, alongside private commercial media, subsidised minority media, media representing political parties and civil society interests, and professional media organisations operating as cooperatives or trusts.[4] A vision of a diverse mix of public, private, and community media, of which public service broadcasting forms part, underlies UNESCO's 'media development indicators' (MDI), drawn up in 2008.[5] Organised into five categories, relating to regulation, diversity, democratic discourse, professional capacity building, and infrastructure, the indicators make up a diagnostic, non-prescriptive toolkit to help identify how far the media in different national settings are being enabled to contribute to democracy and development.

As the UNESCO indicators and allied models recognise, public service media are by no means the sole platform for pluralist and democratic discourse. Yet they are a crucial, and even central, component of what, to use UNESCO terminology, might be judged a 'healthy media ecology'. By definition, public service media are required to give prominence to public affairs, report them impartially, and give space to diverse views from all sections of society and all parts of a country, thereby serving free and open collective public deliberation. In doing so, they should provide a beacon for good journalistic practice. Their purpose is not limited to providing news, current affairs, or documentaries that the market cannot be relied upon to deliver; on the contrary, research shows that the success of a public service operation depends on its ability to compete with commercial bodies in offering general all-round content.[6] However, by applying public service principles of independence from political and commercial pressures, impartiality, inclusivity, and accuracy to the handling of news and information, public service media can help to safeguard 'normative – but increasingly vulnerable – standards of professional journalistic practice and protecting the public interest'.[7]

One achievement of the uprising in 2011 was to demonstrate how large a proportion of Egyptian public opinion refuses to allow a ruling elite to define or determine the public interest. Expression of this refusal called into question significant media-related sections of the country's legislative framework, including the Penal Code and Press Law. In criminalising various types of journalistic reporting, protecting public officials and public bodies from 'criticism', and outlawing advocacy of changes to the constitution, these were already fundamentally at odds with international law.[8]

Far from being resolved after the uprising, these judicial contradictions persisted, as demonstrated by the aforementioned interrogations of journalists and jail sentences for bloggers. In April 2011, for example, a military court invoked Articles 184 and 102 of the Penal Code to sentence blogger Maikel Nabil Sanad to prison for 'insulting the military establishment' and 'spreading false news'. In October 2012, staff from Rotana Masriya were held on charges that they had insulted the judiciary. Thus media workers faced fundamental legal obstacles to developing the media to serve the public interest, in addition to the structural challenge of rehabilitating the government-run press and broadcasting giants bequeathed by Nasser's nationalisation half a century earlier.

This did not stop them trying. Back in 2003 it was possible for the deputy director of news at the ERTU to use the terms 'state' and 'government' interchangeably, as in the assertion that 'TV is state-owned and thus represents the views and policies of the government'.[9] In 2011, journalists inside and outside the ERTU not only challenged that equation, but showed their faith in operational models that would enable print and broadcast media to report 'from the people to the people', independently of government or business. Examination of the proposals and the obstacles they faced can give an idea as to the level of support among Egyptian journalists for public service media and other media categories that treat users primarily as citizens rather than consumers. The discussion in the next section covers categories such as 'civic media', defined as channels of communication linked to organised groups, and 'social market media', defined as minority outlets that can only reach the market through subsidies.[10]

Journalists' initiatives outside the state-run media

Many innovators of media projects in Egypt in 2011 shared the judgement of Ibrahim Gamal el-Din, political science student at the American University in Cairo and co-founder of the Mayadeen Masr News Network, that people had 'lost faith in the media' and were looking for a 'new model' that originates 'from them ... from people who belong to the revolution'.[11] According to its own publicity, the network's purpose was to 'confront the controlled media and cover the news as it is without exaggeration or marginalisation'. The same sense of purpose emerged from countless discussions about the impact of decades of government propaganda on Egyptians' expectations of journalists and the media. The role of the journalist and filmmaker is 'to ask, not to answer' was how Mosireen co-founder, filmmaker, and former Hot Spot Films senior producer Tamer Said expressed it: 'We need to re-educate ourselves, to create a true culture of exposure to thinking. Anything that is not supported or protected by people will not work. The only way is to build a true link with people, by giving them a chance to think and decide.'¹²

Plans for a direct television link from 'the people' to 'the people' were announced in late October 2011 at a press conference in central Cairo, given by three well-known media names on behalf of a larger group of journalists and human rights activists. Together the group said they intended to create a channel called Al-Shaab Yurid, backed by public ownership that was to be achieved through an Initial Public Offering (IPO). Shares were to be sold for £E 10 ($1.65) each, with no single shareholder permitted to own more than 1 per cent of the total value of shares. Co-founder Assad Taha, owner of Hot Spot Films, maker of documentaries for Al-Jazeera, told the press conference that this ownership formula would protect the channel from state intervention as so many backers could not be 'easily targeted by the authorities'.¹³

The announcement came at a moment of particular outrage at government dealings with the media, especially the ERTU's provocative treatment of the Maspero clashes on 9 October and attempted SCAF interference in Yosri Fouda's ONTV show, which led him to suspend it on 21 October. Bilal Fadl, who had recently quit as a presenter for Tahrir TV after its change of direction, said that Yosri Fouda, Mona Shazli, and Mahmoud Saad had all agreed to contribute to the project as individuals, not necessarily as presenters on the future channel. Other backers included Yasser al-Zayat, former managing editor of *Al-Badeel* newspaper and deputy editor of the weekly *Al-Izaa w'al-Telefiziyun* (Radio and Television), and Hussein Abdel-Ghani, former Al-Jazeera bureau chief who had just signed with Al-Nahar TV to host a talkshow called *Akher al-Nahar* (End of the Day) three nights a week. With them were two human rights activists: Gamal Eid of the Arab Network for Human Rights Information and lawyer Amir Salem. According to Fadl, these people had come together because the official media were failing to express the views of the Egyptian people.¹⁴ Besides shielding the channel from business control, the public shareholding initiative would also guarantee 'professionalism and full transparency of the content and the finances of the channel', Fadl said.¹⁵

The journalists had planned to demonstrate to publicise the launch of the IPO, but the Egyptian Financial Supervisory Authority intervened. It warned that permits would be needed not only for the IPO documentation but also for the channel itself. With the ERTU maintaining its monopoly over terrestrial broadcasting and SCAF having frozen licences for new non-government satellite channels the previous month, the prospects for speedy inauguration of Al-Shaab Yurid channel looked remote. The group behind the project said they would put it on hold,[16] which is where it remained more than a year later. Members of the group pointed out that Egypt's renowned nationalist industrialist, Talaat Harb, who founded Bank Misr in 1920 on the principle of selling shares only to Egyptian nationals, would have been unable to do so under the restrictions used to block the IPO for Al-Shaab Yurid channel.

Compared with other initiatives for independent media in 2011, the planned IPO stood out as seeking to fill the public service gap left by the ERTU's status as a government mouthpiece, while also having the potential ultimately to function as an autonomous, journalist-driven exercise in professional 'truth-seeking'.[17] In this it differed from, for example, the planned 'crowd-funding' of the Muslim Brotherhood channel Misr25. Although journalist Hazem Ghurab compared Misr25's subscription-based funding formula with that of broadcasters ranging from National Public Radio in the USA to the public service broadcasters of the UK and Japan, and stressed the channel's mission of professionalism and independence, he also indicated that Misr25 was aimed not at the entire public but at pious Muslims who constituted an untapped advertising market.[18] Taken together, those attributes would place Misr25 in the civic media sector.

Al-Shaab Yurid also offered something other than so-called community media, which may straddle the civic and social market sectors. Egypt has had community radio for several years, but only because enterprising journalists, unable to gain a licence or broadcast frequency, were prepared to launch stations online, sometimes with help from foreign grants. The two earliest ventures were Horytna (Our Freedom), started in 2007, and Banat wa Bas (Girls Only), which followed in 2008. Horytna, seen by supporters as the voice of a new generation fighting for its place in society, set up a tent in Tahrir Square in January 2011 to collate reports on the protests and share them online. The station's own reporter, Mohammed Al-Arabi, was arrested.[19] During parliamentary elections at the end of 2011, Horytna informed Danish youth audiences about Egypt through collaboration with Denmark's public service youth radio station P3. Amani El-Tunisy founded Banat wa Bas as a forum for young women to confront inequality in education, employment, social rights, and political representation. Her station and its team of presenters suffered a setback during the events of early 2011. The Banat wa Bas website states that security forces took away cameras, computers, and other equipment, and detained Tunisy herself for three days, leaving the station more dependent than ever on outside support.[20]

While Horytna and Banat wa Bas fit the profile of minority media requiring external subsidies, two other internet radio stations, launched in 2009, were linked to Egypt's Al-Ghad (Tomorrow) Party, which was officially registered against all the odds after a long political-legal battle in October 2004. Radio Bokra (named after the Egyptian dialect word for 'tomorrow') replaced Al-Ghad Radio, which was closed when the party's leader, Ayman Nour, was sent to prison on fraud charges at the end of 2005, shortly after standing against Mubarak in Egypt's first multi-candidate presidential election. Funded directly through business supporters of Al-Ghad and launched following Nour's release in February 2009, Bokra was intended as a platform for Nour and others to 'offer practical solutions to existing problems', and so 'refute government claims' that opposition groups only criticise and are not able to 'offer alternatives'.[21] Meanwhile, Al-Mahrousa (The Protected One – a term that can refer to 'Egypt' in certain contexts) was presented by its director, April 6 activist Esraa Abdel-Fattah, as having a broader and less partisan agenda, informed by a human rights perspective.

Examples of citizen-oriented projects like those identified here add the weight of action and experience to verbal support from within Egyptian civil society for a diverse and plural media landscape with a public service component. This support was articulated on Press Freedom Day in May 2011 by the National Coalition for Media Freedom (NCMF), formed by 13 organisations and 20 media practitioners. Named individuals behind the coalition included some who later proposed Al-Shaab Yurid, notably Bilal Fadl, Hussein Abdel-Ghani, and Yasser al-Zayat. Among the others were Karem Yehia, an *Al-Ahram* journalist who had founded a 50-strong group called Journalists for Change in 2005 to push for press freedom, an end to jail sentences for journalism 'offences', and the lifting of emergency law. There was also Noura Younis, multimedia editor at *Al-Masry al-Youm* and a prominent blogger since May 2005, when she filed an unsuccessful lawsuit against the police after government-hired thugs attacked and injured her and around 30 other women on a demonstration.

The NCMF's Media Freedom Declaration devoted four paragraphs to urgent action relating to publicly owned media and the features needed to 'rid the Egyptian media' of their 'mono performance'. The declaration said pluralism and diversity were 'pillars of strength' in Egyptian national unity. It called for an end to excessive centralisation of the media in

Cairo and removal of all barriers that deprive Egypt's regions of the 'right to make their own media'. It demanded a review of the 'constitutional, ownership and management patterns' of state-run media institutions as part of a 'phased plan for the rehabilitation of public media', which would equip them to 'do their part as public interest institutions' free from the 'interference of executive authorities, political organisations and parties and pressures of interest groups and influence of advertisers'.[22]

The same four paragraphs also tackled the administrative and legal implications of these demands. They specified that the Ministry of Information and Higher Press Council should be dismantled and replaced with an independent council formed of 'senior professionals, specialists and public figures'. They identified the need to activate audit and monitoring bodies to combat corruption in public media bodies, along with systems for modernising their management and training, to bring them up to 'international standards of transparency, efficiency and productivity'. In order to develop an appropriate legal framework, the Declaration called for all articles restricting media freedom and breaching guarantees of professional practice to be reviewed.[23]

Journalists behind the declaration were among those who protested on 5 October 2011 against a SCAF intervention that would have completely blocked media attempts to serve the public rather than the ruling power. SCAF spokesman Major General Ismail Etman, head of the Armed Forces Department for Army Morale, had notified all newspapers the previous week that nothing should be published about SCAF or the army without written approval from military intelligence and Etman's department. SCAF also designated a military officer to censor content passing through Al-Ahram printing presses, which handle publications from outside the Al-Ahram group. Some 40 leading writers and editors responded by pledging to publish a blank space in place of their usual articles and columns.[24] Etman later seemed to imply that SCAF was backing down on its move, although he persisted with the practice of conflating SCAF's interests with those of the nation at large. He called in to ONTV's prime-time talkshow *Baladna bil-Masry* to deny that SCAF imposes its views on the media, asking only that news coverage should 'respect the national interest'. Etman also urged Yosri Fouda to return to the nightly schedules with his ONTV programme *Akher Kalam*.[25]

The fact that Etman chose to communicate through ONTV testified to his recognition that Egypt's private commercial media enjoy far more credibility than outlets under government control. As discussed in

Chapter 2, private commercial media remained the refuge of journalists who wanted to cover current affairs professionally. Those journalists further demonstrated a commitment to public service when they joined forces across channels to question public figures, as when presenters from Dream and Tahrir TV came together to interview two ruling generals in October 2011. During the 2012 presidential election campaigns, ONTV, Dream, *Al-Masry al-Youm,* and *Al-Shorouk* planned a joint programme of debates. In January 2012, Al-Nahar TV began broadcasting an Arabic translation of the *Doha Debates,* a Qatar Foundation initiative for uncensored public dialogue on critical issues moderated by former BBC journalist and *HardTalk* presenter Tim Sebastian. Speaking for Al-Nahar, Samir Youssef said it was a broadcaster's 'duty' to feature such discussions on a regular basis 'as part of the role in keeping the public informed and encouraging the younger generations to … speak freely'.[26]

Another practical example of public service content was to be found at 25TV, which shunned glitz and highly paid celebrities to give voice to young artists, marginalised constituencies, and people from ordinary poor neighbourhoods, whether in programmes on current affairs, sports, cookery, or the late night talkshow in Ramadan 2012. Unenthusiastic about this kind of content, advertisers stayed away.

Public ownership scenarios for state-run publications

Among those media practitioners and media academics in Egypt who want the country's media to serve the public interest, there are a significant number who believe that, whatever transformation is eventually arrived at for the government-run press, Egypt's longest-surviving newspaper, *Al-Ahram,* should be owned by the public and run by journalists. *Al-Ahram* first appeared in 1876 and, in the assessment of one historian, distinguished itself from the outset by 'putting reportage before political ideology'.[27] A century later the reverse was the case, and by the start of 2011 the newspaper had become a slavish and sycophantic mouthpiece of the regime. Turning it around involves undoing decades of damage caused by corrupt relationships between managers, top editors, and the ruling elite. The process will also be bound up with constitutional changes and a solution for all the other print media under the government's control.

In addition to its broadcasting assets, which are discussed in the next section, the state runs eight media bodies covering 55 publications.

STIMULI FOR A PUBLIC SERVICE ETHOS

Their total workforce has been estimated at 31,000[28] and their debts at £E 10 billion.[29] Al-Ahram Press Organisation is the best known entity, with a staff of some 17,000,[30] a flagship daily newspaper, and a stable of weeklies (in English and French as well as Arabic) and magazines, along with an advertising agency and printing presses. Two other entities publish dailies, namely Dar al-Tahrir with *Al-Gumhuriya* and Dar Akhbar al-Youm with *Al-Akhbar*. Four produce weeklies. They are Dar al-Maarif (*Oktober*), Dar al-Helal (*Al-Musawwar*), Dar al-Shaab (*Al-Rai*), and Dar al-Taawoun (*Al-Siyasi al-Masri*). Of these, Dar al-Helal is seen as standing alongside Al-Ahram as a candidate for future public ownership because of its role in Egypt's cultural heritage. It dates from the 1890s, occupies an historic building in central Cairo, and, through the launching of *Al-Musawwar* (The Illustrated) in 1924, contributed to advancing Egypt's reputation as a regional media centre. The eighth organisation is the Rose el-Youssef establishment, publisher of a daily and weekly of the same name, which has its own board and editorial management.

Under an amendment to the constitution in 1979, all these institutions, along with Egypt's Middle East News Agency (MENA), came under the control of the Higher Press Council, which is appointed by the upper house of Parliament, the Shura Council, itself two-thirds elected and one-third appointed. The Shura Council speaker heads the Higher Press Council. In the new Constitution adopted by referendum in December 2012, Article 216 envisages preserving state-owned publishing houses. It states that a National Association for Press and Media should manage and develop the State-owned press and media institutions, ensuring their 'adherence to sensible professional, administrative and economic standards'.[31] By controlling parliamentary elections and appointments, central government used the 1979 law before 2011 to take control over the choice of board chairman at each media institution and the editor-in-chief of each major publication. Law 96 of 1996 limited the term of chairpersons to four years and that of editors-in-chief to three years, but this did not prevent regular reappointment. Ibrahim Nafie was 71 when he was removed as Al-Ahram board chairman and editor-in-chief of *Al-Ahram* in 2005, after 21 years in the chair, during which time he also served terms as head of the Journalists' Syndicate. Corruption allegations made against Nafie soon after his departure seemed to have central government backing. They suggested that he had lined his own pockets with millions of dollars, despite also receiving a salary equivalent to $0.5 million, which is astronomical in Egyptian terms. High salaries boosted by questionable commissions did not cease in 2005, but corruption cases pursued by *Al-Ahram* staff were investigated at a glacial pace.[32]

In January 2011 the board chairman of Al-Ahram Press Organisation was Abdel-Moneim Said, appointed in 2009, and the editor-in-chief was Osama Saraya, who replaced Nafie in that position in 2005. Said, who had directed the Al-Ahram Centre for Political and Strategic Studies for 15 years at the time of his new appointment, was also a member of NDP's Higher Policy Council, led by Gamal Mubarak. At the start of the protests, Said told the *New York Times* that he could not think of anyone he knew who 'has any concern about the stability of the regime'.[33] That Saraya shared this view was reflected in *Al-Ahram*'s banner headline on 26 January 2011, which was about Lebanon. Saraya had previously overseen the doctoring of a photograph of Mubarak and four other leaders at Middle East peace talks in Washington in September 2010. Instead of the original picture showing US President Barack Obama leading the way on a red carpet, *Al-Ahram*'s version put Mubarak in the lead.

Saraya defended that decision. In an editorial on 17 September, he wrote that the alteration was intended to illustrate Egypt's leading role in the peace process. According to Saraya, the photo was a 'true expression of the prominent stance of President Mubarak in the Palestinian issue, his unique role in leading it before Washington or any other'.[34] This assessment of Mubarak's role was characteristic of *Al-Ahram*'s coverage, as was the edition published on Mubarak's 80th birthday on 4 May 2008, which carried a photograph of the President waving, under the headline 'The day Egypt was born ... anew'. A few months after that edition, Saraya amplified on his admiration for Mubarak during an interview with a Swedish radio journalist. He told her:

> *Don't believe those who sit in cafés and forums and work with the West. Don't believe that they know Egypt. They don't know anything. Hosni Mubarak knows Egypt better than them. ... You cannot believe these young people you talk to ... They don't understand the status of the ruling institution in Egypt. This is an institution that is 7,000 years old. An institution inherited since years. You have to believe that this institution is elected, but elected in a different way than what you know, because this election is 'natural selection'.*[35]

Saraya had difficulty keeping a grip after 26 January, as section editors objected to his editorial line and young staff members downed tools to join the protests in Tahrir Square. He did not attend a large staff meeting on 11 February, the day Mubarak stepped down, at which *Al-Ahram* journalists insisted the paper should apologise to its readers for its coverage. The next day's headline proclaimed 'The People Brought Down the Regime', but Saraya refused to print a letter of apology signed by hundreds of staff.[36] At a press conference on 16 February, convened via Facebook by deputy business editor and video-blogger Sabah Hammamou and others, journalists demanded a new board of directors and editorial council for a transitional period, followed by democratic elections for both bodies. Questioned about these demands by BBC Arabic's Khaled Ezz al-Arab on 17 February, Saraya became so angry he threw his microphone to the floor. 'You are inciting against me. Is that what you're trying to do?', he fumed, and accused the interviewer of trying to undermine stability at *Al-Ahram*.[37]

Essam Sharaf responded to some of the demands, with SCAF's agreement, soon after his appointment as prime minister in March 2011. Said and Saraya were replaced, as were 16 other senior figures across the state-owned publishing houses. But the long-term task of making *Al-Ahram* and the newspapers viable and accountable to the public involved two conflicting objectives: reducing the staff on the one hand; and giving them more of a voice on the other. Even quantifying the scale of the problem was a challenge. In March 2011 the number of reporters at *Al-Ahram* alone was estimated at anywhere between 800 and 1,200, bloated by the way jobs were handed out as favours and sinecures under Mubarak.[38] At that point the most recent financial report, for 2008, apparently showed that *Al-Ahram* had given away $4.3 million worth of jewellery and watches, mobile phones, and electrical appliances to senior political figures and businessmen.[39]

March 2011 was the point at which the roles of the Shura Council and Higher Press Council vis-à-vis the state-run print media, instead of being revised or held in abeyance for future deliberation, were formally perpetuated by the constitutional referendum, which approved a few new clauses but left most of the constitution intact. Technically, if not morally, this legitimated any action by the new Shura Council, elected in February–March 2012, to ensure its control over editorships, exactly as happened under Mubarak. Of the 180 Shura Council seats open for election, 105 went to the Muslim Brothers' Freedom and Justice Party (FJP) and a further 45 to the Salafist party, Nour. In the run-up to the presidential election in May 2012, the Shura Council set about defining criteria for selecting new appointees to the posts of editor-in-chief of some

55 publications, and, soon after Mohammed Morsi was sworn in as president on 30 June, it invited applications for these posts with a deadline of 9 July – a step immediately contested in the courts.

The Shura Council's move put discussion about the economic viability of the state-run press machine on the back burner, focusing attention instead on editorial appointments and who had the right to make them. Applicants were told they should have spent 15 years in the institution, and preferably the publication, where they want to work, and have taken no unpaid leave in the past ten years. (Unpaid leave is the means by which Egyptians augment their income through jobs in the private sector or abroad without sacrificing their public sector position, and the pension and other rights attached to it.) Another stipulation was that they should not have advised the former regime or been involved in normalisation with Israel. Fathy Shehab, head of the Shura Council's information and culture committee, was chosen to oversee selection.

Some 243 journalists submitted applications to the Shura Council, with at least half of the existing editors-in-chief seeking reappointment. Their applications went to a 14-member committee, made up of six Shura Council members, four veteran journalists, and four mass communication professors, although the final decision was reserved for the Shura Council alone. Representatives of the Journalists' Syndicate had already walked out of talks about the selection process – some because they rejected Shura Council involvement and others because they objected to non-professionals making the choice. Journalists held an emergency meeting at the Syndicate building on 7 July, in the absence of Syndicate chairman, Mamdouh el-Waly. Waly, a Muslim Brotherhood ally who was freely elected as chairman the previous October, excused himself on the grounds that he needed to negotiate with Shura Council speaker, Ahmad Fahmy, about the appointment committee's composition.[40] On 8 July hundreds of journalists gathered in front of Al-Ahram building and marched in protest to the Shura Council.

The action by elected FJP members of the Shura Council gave the distinct impression that the group behind the FJP, the Muslim Brotherhood, wanted to secure their influence over the press while there was still time. With the future of the upper house of Parliament in some doubt after the Supreme Constitutional Council ruled in June that elections to the lower house of Parliament were partially invalid, and with a new constitution yet to be drafted, the FJP's window of opportunity for benefiting from the 1979 editorial appointment procedure looked limited. Hamdeen Sabahi, who came third in the first round of presidential elections, used his Facebook page to urge postponing the press appointments until the Shura Council's future role was fully decided. Sabahi, with a background in journalism, said he supported loosening the government's grip on the press.

When they were announced, in two stages in August and September 2012, the Shura Council appointments proved controversial. The candidate selected as chief editor of *Al-Ahram*, Abdel-Nasser Salama, the paper's former bureau chief in Muscat, Oman, allegedly failed the requirement for ten years' uninterrupted service. Moreover, the paper had suspended his weekly column in 2010 after he accused the Coptic Pope Shenouda of inciting sectarian strife. Yasser Rizk, editor of *Al-Akhbar*, was removed in favour of Mohammed Hassan al-Banna, grandson of the Muslim Brotherhood's founder. The fact that Rizk was instantly appointed as chief editor of *Al-Masry al-Youm*, to fill the vacancy left by Magdi Galad earlier in the year, indicated a level of professional respect for his achievements that the Shura Council apparently did not share. Gamal Abdel-Rahim, appointed editor of *Al-Gumhuriya*, had attracted condemnation from Egyptian human rights organisations in 2009 for statements he made on a TV programme and in *Al-Gumhuriya* that were interpreted as condoning attacks on members of the Bahai minority religious sect.[41]

The Shura Council's decision to select new heads of state-run publications was far from the editorial overhaul that many journalists in those publications and the Middle East News Agency (MENA) felt to be long overdue. *Al-Ahram*'s previous post-revolution board chairman, Abdel-Fattah El-Gebaly, and its deputy editor-in-chief, Mohammed Sabreen, went through the motions of discussing 'Media in Transition' at a seminar on 13 November 2011. But staff in attendance complained that the newspaper still seemed to owe allegiance to the government, citing its silence on topics such as military trials of civilians, and they openly called for changes at the top.[42]

AhramOnline editor (and former editor of *Al-Ahram Weekly*[43]) Hani Shukrallah highlighted the persistent presence in the media of 'state security guards' from the Mubarak era, during an interview in October 2011. He told AUC Press at a book launch:

> *The main state security man on the Al-Ahram staff – very powerful, everybody was afraid of him – was one of the people behind my being fired from Al-Ahram Weekly. During the revolution he was justifying the killing of demonstrators and today he is in the same position – deputy editor of Al-Ahram.*[44]

During the presidential election campaign in 2012, MENA journalists complained to the Shura Council as well as the Higher Press Council and the Culture and Media Committee at the People's Assembly that their editor-in-chief, El-Sayed Adel Abdel-Aziz, was using the agency to support the candidacy of Ahmad Shafik. The Cairo-based Arab Network for Human Rights Information issued a statement drawing attention to these alleged violations and calling for urgent reform and restructuring of state press institutions. It said these were still controlled by 'hidden' security services and interest groups, which worked together to impede any attempt to develop them professionally as a means of expression for the general public.[45]

Legally, the possibility did exist for the state-run press to be transformed into public service media outlets, run by independent governing boards. Under the Press Law, the state-run newspapers are intended to be 'free-standing and autonomous', providing a 'free national platform for all political voices and trends and key actors'.[46] Numerous reform proposals acknowledged that they cannot be autonomous if editors are appointed by the majority party in the Shura Council. Less than two months after Mubarak's removal, at a conference sponsored by the Ministry of Culture under the title 'Rebuilding Egyptian Media for a Democratic Future', university academics and media practitioners from across Egypt called jointly for newspapers to be transferred to public ownership in the form of 'publicly listed shareholding institutions that all Egyptians have a right to own, oversee and hold accountable in terms of budgets, editorial policy and ethics'. They wanted the Egyptian public not only to own but also to be able to manage print media organisations, through elected editorial boards and boards of trustees.[47]

Variations on the themes of publicly owned shares and elections emerged in subsequent proposals. Independent journalist and editor Ibrahim Eissa said on 3 June 2011: 'As a journalist I am against the selling of *Al-Ahram*; I support the idea that it should be for the people and owned by its workers.'[48] Yasser al-Zayat, a journalism trainer and backer of the project Al-Shaab Yurid, said ownership of the press institutions should be transferred 'to the people', with general assemblies of each one electing their own board, which would appoint editors-in-chief.[49] However, some other suggestions begged the question of how many employees the state-run newspapers could afford to keep. Abdel-Wahab Ads, speaking as deputy editor-in-chief of *El-Gumhuriya* in July 2012, suggested that 51 per cent of each newspaper's stock should belong to the employees and the rest be put up for public subscription.[50] Salah Eissa, secretary general of the Higher Press Council, also envisaged employees owning half their institution as a possible scenario.[51] Employee share ownership, as envisaged in these proposals, implied likely resistance to any dramatic downsizing of the press organisations.

Support for an independent ERTU

Public service broadcasting is unfamiliar to Egyptians, either as a concept or practice. Part of the reason lies in the different political contexts in which broadcasting evolved in Europe, especially the UK, compared with Arab countries that were under British, French, or Italian control. In the UK in the 1920s there was political pressure for broadcasting to be treated as a public utility that would serve the democratic process. In Egypt, unlicensed commercial and amateur radio services that existed in the 1920s were closed by government decree in 1931. When radio started up again in 1934 it was operated by the UK firm Marconi with an 'unmistakably British' tone, until the Marconi contract was cancelled in 1947 and ownership and operation was taken into Egyptian hands.[52] Responsibility for radio then passed between the ministries of interior and social affairs until the military took over in 1952, after which Nasser began to deploy radio as a propaganda tool to mobilise support for his Arab nationalist project. Voice of the Arabs, which quickly became a full-scale broadcasting service with powerful transmitters, began life as a programme on Cairo Radio in 1953.

Television was launched with a speech by Nasser in 1960, on the anniversary of the 1952 revolution, as part of the same one-party, nationalist mission. It was placed under the Ministry of National Guidance – renamed Ministry of Information in 1969. Since news bulletins followed government orders, offering uncritical, unquestioning, and sometimes false accounts of activities by the military leadership, the public was unprepared for the reality of Egypt's crushing defeat and loss of territory in the 1967 Arab–Israeli war. Radio, television, and broadcast engineering were brought together under one roof as the Egyptian Radio and Television Union (ERTU) in 1971, and a special law, passed in 1979, gave the ERTU a monopoly over terrestrial broadcasting, with Articles 5–10 putting it under presidential and information ministry control. Law 223 of 1989 amended that law to make the information minister's role in ERTU governance structures even more central.[53]

In other words, neither the ERTU nor its predecessors operated as a public service. Instead, the very notion of 'publicness' was tainted by its long association with the inefficient and discredited 'public sector' created in Egypt by wholesale nationalisation. When translated into Arabic, the term 'public service broadcasting' needs to be amended to 'broadcasting to serve the citizen' (*izaa fi khidmat al-muwaten*) to carry at least some of the same meaning. In the same way, the history of Egyptian institutions has led to the term 'state' being connected in ordinary parlance more closely with an authoritarian form of government than with the concept of a public power that is above and beyond the government of the day, enjoying continuity that the government should not. For that reason, any hint that broadcasting should be subject to 'state regulation' is today contentious, not least because the Arabic word commonly used for 'regulation' also has connotations of censorship.

Despite all of that, the aftermath of Mubarak's overthrow witnessed an abundance of projects aimed in one way or another at endowing the ERTU with characteristics of a public service broadcaster in the UNESCO sense of the term. UNESCO criteria, outlined in 2005, are: universality (meaning the entire population has full access to the service in terms of technical reception, interest, and understanding); diversity (in the programmes offered, the audiences targeted, and the subjects discussed); independence (guaranteed through protection from political and commercial pressures); and distinctiveness (through a remit to innovate and set high standards).[54] Actions aimed at promoting one or more of these four elements originated both inside and outside the ERTU. In some cases they reflected commitments that had been made by the ERTU's own management in previous years.

Approaches to journalism within the ERTU have to be seen in the context not only of its history, sketched out above, but also of who runs news production and how it is organised. The organisation has a workforce of 43,000[55] for the same reasons as the state-run press has around 31,000; namely that massive overstaffing in state organisations, partly driven by nepotism, traditionally helped to mask real unemployment rates. The ERTU has nine departments, which ERTU staff refer to in English as 'sectors', dealing separately with finance, engineering, radio, television, satellite television, and so on. One of these sectors is responsible for 'News' and another for the digital Nile Thematic Network that was formed, complete with its own Nile News channel, in 1998. In around 2008, management of the two news operations was unified under a new head of the News Sector, who had been appointed in 2005. Unusually, the appointee came from outside the ERTU. He was Abdel-Latif el-Menawy, who until then worked for the Saudi-owned *Asharq al-Awsat* newspaper in London.

Menawy, an NDP member, has said that he took the ERTU job because he wanted to reform the ERTU from within. In his book, *Tahrir: The Last 18 Days of Mubarak*, he recounts that his 'idea was to turn state television into public television'.[56] Judging from the ERTU's coverage during the '18 days', which caused senior staff to walk out in disgust and made Menawy's position so difficult that he could only enter and exit the building on 13–14 February under armed escort, the reform project did not progress very far. AUC journalism professor Naila Hamdy compared the ERTU's reporting of the uprising in 2011 with the falsehoods put out by government television during the 1967 war. People alive then 'still don't trust the state media to this day', she said. In the events of January–February 2011 it was not a case of 'one errant report or a single misquote; this was the creation of a completely parallel reality'.[57]

What Menawy actually meant by the phrase 'public television' during his time in office is unclear. Interviewed by the *Guardian*'s Jack Shenker, he suggested that public television 'will always be the eye of the public'.[58] Yet his book recounts the frequency with which he requested permission from Minister of Information Anas el-Fiqi, Gamal Mubarak, and top NDP officials before running a programme – requests that were often refused.[59] Interviewed by Stephen Sackur for the BBC's *HardTalk* programme, Menawy insisted that he was working 'for the nation, not for a person or a regime', and argued that ERTU coverage of the 2005 presidential election was 'the best', the 'most balanced', at the time.[60] Yet the Cairo Institute for Human Rights Studies monitored coverage on Egypt TV Channels 1, 2, and 3 as well as Nile News during the first week of that election campaign, and found that state-owned channels allotted far more time to Mubarak than any of his nine rivals.[61] For Hala Hashish, head of Nile News in 2005, ERTU was undoubtedly 'government TV'. She believed no other 'government in the world would have ... welcomed everyone to come and criticize the government on its own TV stations'.[62] Hala Hashish remained as head of the Nile Television Network in 2011 after Menawy left.

Menawy's confidence that ERTU news was serving 'the public and not the state or the government'[63] was openly contested by ERTU staff immediately after Mubarak's downfall, when they formally complained to the Prosecutor General that £E 11 billion ($1.8 billion) of public money

– the size of the ERTU deficit – had been squandered since 2000 by the information minister, the ERTU chairman, and the head of news.[64] Employees also came together to call for a minimum wage of £E 2,000, new contracts, and for heads of department to be chosen by election.[65] A further strand of activism emerged, focused on abolishing the information ministry and developing policy recommendations to make the ERTU independent. These efforts had a faltering start in March 2011, but were revitalised after the attacks on Coptic demonstrators outside Maspero on 9 October 2011, when many wanted urgently to distance themselves from ERTU coverage of the violence.[66]

One group, the Media Revolutionaries Front, consisting of presenters, reporters, directors, and photographers, held discreet meetings to devise forms of representation that would be effective enough to expose state security interference and pressure the government to reform the state media. Another group, describing itself as a coalition of Independent Media Professionals, diagnosed self-censorship as a serious obstacle. Dalia Hassouna, a state radio anchor behind the coalition, said: 'Most of the people are either loyal to the old regime or they were hired through nepotism, not based on their caliber, and so they are grateful to those who hired them, which means they would do anything they are asked.'[67] Sheer numbers of employees magnified the significance of this challenge. At the start of 2011, between 3,000 and 3,500 people reported to Menawy as head of news.[68] Menawy says he 'only needed' 350 and 'really worked' with fewer than 100.[69]

With the appointment of Ahmad Anis as information minister, Nile News staff launched an open-ended strike to protest at the pro-SCAF policies of old and new managers and demand that Nile News should be given independence from the ERTU News Sector. Nile News's Hedi Sameh explained: 'We want to be free from their shame.'[70] Ibrahim El-Mergawi, who placed a banner saying 'Freedom for Nile News' on a studio set in February 2012, was disciplined, reportedly on the instructions of Anis and Menawy's replacement as head of news, Ibrahim Kamel el-Sayed.

ERTU coverage of the Maspero violence rekindled turmoil inside the organisation, but it also triggered a reminder from an international body that the ERTU had made its own voluntary commitment to 'independent reporting', which it needed to observe. Because of the way the International Telecommunication Union defines world regions, the ERTU is one of several Arab national broadcasters eligible to belong to the European Broadcasting Union (EBU). But EBU membership carries certain obligations, which are very similar to the criteria of public service broadcasting outlined by UNESCO.[71] The EBU was so concerned at reports of ERTU anchors urging viewers to side with the military during the 9 October demonstration that its president and director general wrote to the ERTU chairman, Tharwat Mekki, reminding him that EBU membership 'entails a commitment to independent and impartial reporting at the service of all sections of the population, including minorities'.[72]

Since EBU membership is optional, the obligations it carries have to be regarded as originating from inside the member organisation, not as an external or foreign imposition. The same applies to ERTU membership of the Conference of Mediterranean Audiovisual Operators (COPEAM), of which the ERTU was actually a founder member at COPEAM's inaugural meeting, hosted in Cairo in 1996. In 2005, COPEAM issued the Seville Charter, which it described as the first document to affirm the ethical professional values shared by broadcasters on both shores of the Mediterranean. The Charter echoed elements of the public service remit espoused by UNESCO and the EBU. Intended to reinforce a 'framework of respect, tolerance and dialogue', it committed its signatories to respect pluralism of opinions, show responsibility, fairness, accuracy, and objectivity in reporting facts and events, and 'abstain from any form of misinformation through omissions'.[73] The ERTU was among the first COPEAM members to sign the Seville Charter in May 2005 and it hosted COPEAM's annual conference in April 2009.

Objectivity and pluralism were still missing from the ERTU's main evening news bulletin and prime-time political talkshows during parliamentary election coverage in November–December 2011. AUC journalism professor Rasha Abdallah, who monitored the output, found a 'great deal' of improvement in regional coverage, in contrast to the previous practice of focusing solely on Cairo. She also found more diversity than previously in the identities of talkshow guests. Despite these changes, however, news items were ordered according to political protocol, with military generals featuring in lead stories with no news value, soldiers pictured only in favourable situations, and occasional editorialising on the part of anchors. Women and religious minorities barely featured in either news bulletins or talkshows.[74]

This mixed outcome seems to reflect one of the difficulties facing ERTU journalists who support independent news coverage, with inclusivity and balance in news reports: namely, improvement efforts are piecemeal and not part of the systematic overhaul that groups like the

Independent Media Professionals want. Recent years have seen various training programmes provided by foreign news organisations, aimed at bringing ERTU news reporting closer to international norms. For ERTU managers such exercises were often a case of mere lip service, driven more by a desire to stay on good terms with Western donors than to overhaul local practices and thereby disturb political hierarchies. Outsiders report that ERTU trainees are eager to 'know', 'engage', 'learn new things', 'discuss', and 'apply universal principles of fair play'.[75] Yet the change of regime in 2011 did not instantly remove the obstacles blocking independent reporting, even at a micro level, such as entrenched restrictions, antiquated ancillary services, or indifference from senior management. Restrictions included the need for written permission to film in the street or outside Cairo, or even to use the archives. As someone who enjoyed teaching video-journalism to Nile News reporters put it: 'When the [right] conditions were there to do the story, they did it. What you can't control is all the other conditions surrounding them.'[76]

The BBC World Service Trust, now known as BBC Media Action, worked with the ERTU on a mission statement, editorial guidelines, and a style guide in 2006-7. The guidelines up to that point were far from conducive to fair and inclusive reporting. On the contrary, a set of 33 ethical principles' consisted mainly of prohibitions on any kind of critical thinking or engagement with important social or political issues. Examples include: 'It is prohibited to broadcast any program that criticizes state officials because of their performance'; and 'It is prohibited to broadcast any program that creates social confusion or criticizes the principles and traditions of Arab society'.[77] An ERTU staff member who trained with the BBC in September 2006 recounted how it 'dawned' on him and his colleagues that they were 'amateurs' working for a 'kind of media that has nothing to do with professionalism'.[78]

When new editorial guidelines were drawn up, using the BBC template for reference, Ahmad Mamdouh Hassan, Nile News Supervisor for Editorial Matters, hinted that their acceptance had not been secured. Hassan wrote in the World Service Trust *Annual Review* that he hoped they would be 'adopted soon so that all those who work for Egyptian TV can benefit'.[79] Whatever the editorial guidelines said, they were not much in evidence in 2011-12, when ERTU teams took part in training on election coverage. In one project in mid-2011, the British Embassy in Cairo sponsored an independent consultant to facilitate the drafting of guidelines for election coverage by a combined team of ten news editors

STIMULI FOR A PUBLIC SERVICE ETHOS

from ERTU News and Nile News. The new head of news, Ibrahim Kamel El-Sayed, endorsed the drafting process and promised to circulate the final text throughout the ERTU. In another, BBC Media Action and BBC Arabic's Cairo bureau worked with 160 staff from ERTU national and regional channels in November 2011 to prepare them for what a headline in *Al-Shorouk* called the ERTU's 'election exam'.

The same BBC partners were also funded by the Foreign Office under the Arab Partnership Participation Fund to carry out another project aimed at making the ERTU more like a public service broadcaster. This was *Sa'at Hissab* (Hour of Reckoning), a format based on the BBC's *Question Time*, which airs each week from a different location in the UK, hosting panellists from the fields of politics, business, and civil society, answering questions put by a studio audience. In the end, because dealings with the ERTU became more inflexible in 2012 after Ahmad Anis was appointed as information minister, one episode of *Sa'at Hissab* was co-produced with a private channel, Al-Hayat, instead.[80] But one was co-produced with the ERTU's Channel 7, a regional channel. It took place in Minya, with a 240-strong audience from all the governorates in Upper Egypt, who challenged governorate officials on security, education, fuel shortages, and military rule. By wanting to continue the programme after the recording was over, and refusing to leave, the audience members showed the level of public demand for an independent broadcaster that serves citizens, not the ruling elite.

Implications for journalism in the private commercial sector

Journalism financed by private commercial companies has become such a prominent and established feature of Egypt's media landscape that questions about the business models behind it are rarely asked. Yet, based on past experience, there is concern that any eventual overhaul of state-run media will be conducted without regard to the full implications for financial sustainability of journalism in both the public and private sectors. In the 1990s, before the Mubarak regime finally announced the concession whereby private investors were permitted to broadcast by satellite from a designated zone, one of the government's own advisers warned it against 'slouching toward privatization' and 'leaving the future to be settled by inadvertence'.[81]

It is a moot point whether the brevity and vague wording of the licensing arrangements put in place for locally incorporated private satellite broadcasters in 2000 were intentional or inadvertent. Either way, they neglected to remove the state broadcaster's monopoly on terrestrial transmission and made a general investment agency, the General Authority for Investment (GAFI), responsible for the oversight of content transmitted. Just as the legal requirement that anyone wanting to publish a daily newspaper in Egypt should supply a £E 1 million ($164,000) deposit, together with the names of nine business partners, kept newspaper publishing out of reach of anyone not favoured by the dictatorship, so broadcasting was effectively reserved for the same business elite – people who could cross-subsidise media ventures from other parts of their business empires. These were people who initially accepted, under the terms of their licence, not to challenge taboos on political coverage, even though their channels needed to be relevant and interesting to Egyptian audiences if they were to be economically viable.

Journalism has thus developed in the private commercial sector in the face of serious legal obstacles. As ONTV director Albert Shafik explained in September 2011, for a private commercial broadcaster to air live news of any kind was to defy the authorities because most broadcast licences did not allow it. ONTV had started to do this before the revolution, he said, but it was a 'very risky and dangerous move' that provoked persistent warning letters and problems from the licensing body. ONTV was trying to 'play the role that Egyptian state TV couldn't play', Shafik said, by creating a 'leading news channel'.[82] Indeed, ONTV and Dream TV were playing a role that the literature on Egypt's uprising has sometimes attributed to Al-Jazeera, even though Egyptian viewership of Al-Jazeera had already diminished dramatically by 2009.

Aref Hijjawi, who, as Programme Director at Al-Jazeera's Arabic channel, saw the audience survey data produced in 2009, concedes that Egyptian viewership of Al-Jazeera may have inched up again after the pre-election clampdown on Egypt's private channels in 2010.[83] But neither Hijjawi, nor Wadah Khanfar, who was director general of the Al-Jazeera Network until September 2011, believe Al-Jazeera's coverage played any part in Egyptian actions when the uprising started. On the contrary, 23 January 2011 saw Al-Jazeera Arabic begin four days of blanket coverage on the Palestine Papers, detailing negotiations between the Palestinian Authority and Israel. Coverage suddenly switched to Egypt on the third day, when Al-Jazeera staff discovered that pan-Arab viewers, alert to events in Egypt, were searching other sources for information about them. Overwhelmed by the demands of coverage with so few Al-Jazeera staff on the ground in Egypt, Khanfar later told Harvard University's Berkman Center for Internet and Society that he decided to air citizen reports coming in over the internet via Facebook and Twitter, setting aside his editors' concerns about authentication.[84] According to Hijjawi, Al-Jazeera 'reassured the revolutionaries' by being 'very clear and immutable in its pro-rebellion stance'.[85] Yet a pivotal moment such as Mona Shazli's interview with Wael Ghoneim (see Chapter 1) on 7 February 2011, which is credited with swelling and reinforcing the protest against the regime,[86] took place on Dream 2, an Egyptian channel.

As the ONTV and Dream 2 examples show, the process of testing legal boundaries depended before and after Mubarak's overthrow on the unpredictable perseverance and fluctuating political clout of individual media owners. The haphazard results were summed up by Magdi Abdel-Hadi, the BBC's former Arab affairs analyst, at the end of 2011. He told the *Financial Times*: 'Egypt's media are like the rest of the country: chaotic, devoid of standards, full of energy with no sense of direction.'[87] In late 2012, Morsi's government showed it was ready to go into battle with long-established private networks when it notified Dream TV that it should relocate its operations, so as to uplink to Nilesat from inside Media Production City rather than outside it. Shortly before the notification a leading figure in the Muslim Brotherhood's Freedom and Justice Party had raised a case against Gehan Mansour, an anchor at Dream TV, for describing him as a 'fascist politician'. Bahgat offered evidence that Dream TV's location had been sanctioned under Mubarak, but the information minister, Salah Abdel-Maqsoud, insisted that these arrangements had expired and were now illegal. Bahgat's response was to suspend broadcasts, screening only a disclaimer blaming the government for Dream TV's programmes being off air. State media accounts of the dispute implied that Bahgat was depriving state coffers of much-needed revenue by operating outside Media Production City.

When the state media's financial woes are added to the mix of factors creating unpredictability for private commercial media, prospects for resolving deficiencies in the regulatory framework look distant. In July 2012 the ERTU was so close to bankruptcy it had to be rescued with an emergency injection of £E 200 million ($33 million), shared equally between the state and the National Investment Bank, in order to pay salaries that were overdue. Two days later there were hints that the government would seek to recover some of the outgoings by increasing the tiny levy for broadcasting included in electricity bills. The levy had remained unchanged at two piastres (£E 1=100 piastres) since the 1970s. The rise would have to be considerable, however, to meet the situation that Salah Abdel-Maqsoud described to one interviewer shortly after his appointment as information minister. He said that the information ministry, responsible for the ERTU, was paying salaries at a rate of £E 225 million per year and, besides its debts to the National Investment Bank, owed another £E 850 million to news agencies, photographic agencies, and production companies.[88]

Under pressure to improve their balance sheets, state-run media may be reluctant to surrender the shares of advertising revenue they have traditionally enjoyed through political manipulation, or to give up the printing and distribution that state publishing houses undertake for the privately owned press. It was revealed in August 2011 that the ERTU relied on independent production houses to bring advertising along with their productions, to enable Egypt state TV to take a percentage. This was on top of the system whereby advertising spend with state TV could be exempted from taxes that are incurred when advertising is placed with privately owned outlets.

Commentators have rightly pointed out the challenge of establishing what is meant by free speech in post-Mubarak Egypt. One summed it up as a problem of how to 'distinguish between shrill and seditious; between vitriol and violence; between loose talk and libel; and among professionalism, patronage, and politics in state-owned media'.[89] Abdel-Maqsoud himself focused on questions of ethics in interviews about his intentions as information minister. But the task of agreeing such boundaries looked like the easy option compared to the gargantuan project of structural reform. Such a project is needed to achieve a more equitable share of resources between state-run media and those private companies that have been delivering some of the public service content that state bodies would normally be expected to provide.

4

Nuts and Bolts of a New Deal

> Pending implementation of Egypt's international commitments on trade union pluralism, many journalists feel their rights are underprotected. The task has fallen to individuals to work with media owners to set editorial standards inside organisations and create cross-cutting professional networks to promote good practice in both management and journalism. This kind of capacity building calls for liberalisation of laws on freedom of association.

All over the world, institutional models for representing journalists and safeguarding good journalism are in flux. Multimedia convergence calls for a fundamental rethink of ways to promote ethical and quality content across all delivery platforms: text, audio, and image, online as well as offline. According to the International Federation of Journalists (IFJ), journalists' unions everywhere are adjusting to the changing media landscape by 'renovating their recruitment and organising objectives'.[1] Questions about the relative emphasis on professional approaches, as distinct from legal ones, are central to the renovation process. Aidan White, former IFJ general secretary, distinguishes between 'bureaucratic frameworks for policing journalism' and a 'new vision' that 'encourages self-regulation as a positive force for setting high standards and defending them'. Legal guarantees may be beneficial, White argues, but will be more sustainable if 'cast in the mould of self-rule'.[2]

Policing of journalism in Egypt in the early post-Mubarak era continued to invoke laws that restrict formal representation of media professionals, as well as the content they produce. This creates a double bind. Journalists have to abide by legal means of representation if they want to resist other media laws, as a telling example from the 1990s can illustrate. The Journalists' Syndicate, the statutory sole representative body for the profession, mobilised so effectively against Law No. 93 of 1995, which contained draconian amendments to the 1980 press law, that the measure was repealed. Even though its replacement, Law No. 96 of 1996, was only marginally less illiberal, the mobilisation cast the Syndicate in a positive light as a united force for demanding acceptable basic conditions for journalism. Yet the Syndicate's success was also clearly linked to its close relationship to the government, embodied in the large number of its members working for the state-run press. Most notable of these was Ibrahim Nafie, head of both the Syndicate and Al-Ahram Press Organisation. The harsher its restrictions on the press, the more the government antagonised its own allies and employees.[3]

A classic example like this clearly exposes the web of questionable interconnections – not only between the mechanism for professional representation and the possibility of influencing media laws, but also between the representative body and the extent of media ownership in government hands. That is to say: the process of setting and defending high standards for journalism in Egypt faces entrenched and interlinked structural hurdles. Tackling the hurdles in turn raises questions of principle about union formation and membership, and issues of governance inside media organisations. The hurdles also impinge on the effectiveness of technical and financial support for journalism development, an area of interest to foreign donors.

Egypt's trade unions, previously forced to belong to the Egyptian Trade Union Federation (ETUF), have historically been separate from its professional syndicates, but both have in common a history of monopoly status, in contravention of two International Labour Organisation (ILO) conventions, which Egypt has signed and ratified. ILO Convention No. 87, on Freedom of Association and Protection of the Right to Organise, and No. 98, on the Right to Organise and Collective Bargaining, have the status of international treaties. Therefore, according to Ahmad Hassan al-Borei, a labour law professor who was manpower minister in the shortlived cabinet of Essam Sharaf, they supersede national restrictions on the formation of labour unions. Speaking on a panel at the Journalists' Syndicate in March 2011, Borei promised that workers would soon have

> the right to establish, form and join any trade union of their choice – trade unions which would remain completely independent of the ministry. These unions would be able to independently conduct their domestic affairs, develop regulations, allocate their funds and choose their own leaders.[4]

By the time Borei made his promise, Egypt already had a rival to ETUF, in the form of the Egyptian Federation of Independent Trade Unions (EFITU), created as part of the uprising on 30 January 2011. EFITU brought together breakaway unions and syndicates representing teachers, health technicians, and others, including the Independent General Union of Real Estate Tax Authority Workers (IGURETA), which had started the breakaway trend two years earlier. When the People's Assembly eventually convened at the start of 2012, dominated by the Muslim Brotherhood's Freedom and Justice Party (FJP), it considered a law drafted by Borei, which would accord recognition to non-ETUF unions, authorise any group of 50 or more workers to form a union, and permit multiple unions in a single workplace. However, ETUF resisted the loss of its monopoly status and the FJP opted for a compromise that failed to meet ILO standards. It accepted to legalise non-ETUF unions, but wanted a limit of only one trade union in an enterprise. Parliament was dissolved in June 2012. But the signs were that SCAF was not prepared to permit free association of workers and that the Muslim Brotherhood would only back reform of trade union legislation within certain limits.[5]

Developments within the Journalists' Syndicate and alternative mobilisation platforms for labour organisation in Egypt's wider media community can thus be assessed against international standards and the groundswell of the country's burgeoning union movement. In the upheaval of 2011, with national laws in contention, especially those that contradict UN human rights guarantees, workers seized opportunities to set precedents. The formation in October 2011 of a second independent trade movement, the Egyptian Democratic Labour Congress (EDLC), reflected the breadth and depth of unionisation initiatives across many sectors, including the media. At the same time, a sudden expansion in the number of privately operated media outlets, many of them electronic, boosted the number and diversity of media workers in need of union protection. Recognition of the urgent need for labour law reform seemed implicit in the choice of speakers at the Journalists' Syndicate conference to mark World Press Freedom Day on 3 May 2011. The opening panel featured IGURETA activist Kamal Abu Aita and Justice Tehany El-Gebaly, Egypt's first woman judge (appointed in 2003) and vice-president of the Supreme Constitutional Court.

Unionisation in a legal limbo

The Journalists' Syndicate is a mandatory, statutory union that is exclusive to journalists in the print media. Egypt has 24 professional syndicates, which were traditionally separated from trade unions by several means, including a stipulation that a new professional syndicate can only be formed with People's Assembly approval and must not serve a profession for which a syndicate already exists.[6] The Mubarak regime tightened its grip over syndicate boards even further in 1993 by means of a law (No. 100) that invalidated any internal election conducted with a turnout below 50 per cent. For syndicates with over a million members, this stipulation was impossible to achieve. Fifteen years after its introduction, the Supreme Constitutional Court struck down Law No. 100, just weeks before Mubarak was removed.[7]

The Journalists' Syndicate was given its legal status in Nasser's day, by Law No. 76 of 1970. The law recognises four categories of journalist: working, unemployed, affiliated, or under apprenticeship.[8] Article 7 requires journalists to have completed a prescribed apprenticeship in order to qualify for 'employed' status, which Article 6 defines as 'regular paid employment' with 'regular and fixed' remuneration. The Syndicate is not open to journalists in the broadcast media and there is no mention of freelance journalism. Nor is it clear that Article 12, which authorises the Registration Committee to grant affiliate status to individuals who fail to meet the membership conditions set out in Article 5, resolves the freelance issue, since 'regular paid employment' is not one of the conditions listed in Article 5.[9] The rules give any journalist wishing to obtain a contract of employment in order to qualify for Syndicate membership an incentive to prioritise an editor's whims over the demands of professionalism. The system of licensing gave the Mubarak regime an additional weapon against any unregistered journalist whose work annoyed the ruling political and business elite.

For these and other reasons the true percentage of the total number of Egyptian journalists who are served by the Syndicate is much smaller than the usually quoted ratio of 6,000 members out of a potential 'eligible' pool of 14,000. Broadcast and most online journalists are not eligible. Journalists from non-government newspapers were routinely denied entry under the old regime. In one round of applications in 2008, scores of candidates from *Al-Ghad*, *El-Destour*, and *Al-Badeel* complained that they had been asked questions about their political opinions, after which their applications were rejected, whereas no one applying from a state-run publication was turned down.¹⁰ Without membership, journalists lack accreditation to access government press conferences, interview freely, or receive the monthly salary supplement that Makram Mohammed Ahmad put in place after being elected to chair the Syndicate in 2007. Apparently with government approval, Ahmad had promised a monthly supplement of £E 200 ($33) to every member as part of his election campaign.¹¹ He focused again on cost-of-living issues when standing for re-election in 2009 and some sources say the payments had increased to £E 600 per month by 2011.¹²

After Mubarak's removal, journalists in different fields demonstrated their dissatisfaction with the role of the Journalists' Syndicate and its practices by forming alternative groups that would represent practitioners, and set professional standards in more independent and flexible ways. The first to be announced, on 22 April 2011, was the Independent Journalists' Syndicate. Co-founded by Wael Tawfik, an activist from a group calling itself Journalists Without a Syndicate, Shaimaa Galal and others, the new independent body claimed more than 300 members, around one-fifth of whom reportedly also had membership in the official Journalists' Syndicate.¹³ The latter body acted immediately to protect its legal monopoly. It filed a complaint with the Public Prosecutor, citing the law that requires any new syndicate to be established by an Act of Parliament. Sayyed Abu Zeid, legal adviser to the Journalists' Syndicate, said the new body would 'only serve to divide the ranks of Egypt's journalists'. 'I support plurality for political parties', he said, 'but not for syndicates. Journalists have common interests; we should unite to protect our interests'.¹⁴

The Journalists' Syndicate was arguably more accommodating to the second new entity, the Syndicate of Electronic Journalists. Salah Abdel-Sabour, secretary general of the Arab Union for Electronic Journalists and a journalist at the Saudi-owned portal MBC.net, led the founding committee for the union for online journalists in Egypt, based on discussions that started in 2010, if not earlier.¹⁵ The rationale for this project lay in the fact that the Journalists' Syndicate would only admit online journalists who worked with newspapers that produced a paper version as well as an electronic one. Interviewed alongside Abdel-Sabour on the Nile Culture channel on 6 December 2011, Ahmad Aboul-Qassem, general secretary of the Syndicate of Electronic Journalists, said his group was ready to cooperate with any other union, but admitted that there had been no cooperation with the Journalists' Syndicate so far. The two interviewees pointed out that the latter's recently elected head, Mamdouh el-Waly, had acknowledged the need to change the Syndicate's rules in order to keep up with the times vis-à-vis online journalism. Even so, they said he might face resistance from the Syndicate's General Assembly.[16]

Broadcast journalists also used the aftermath of Mubarak's overthrow to try to organise representation for themselves. Their exclusion from the Journalists' Syndicate, a side effect of the government's monopoly over terrestrial broadcasting, was already a long-standing point of contention. When privately owned satellite stations such as Dream and El-Mehwar were first licensed in 2001-2, their most prominent presenters also had careers as print journalists and were generally eligible for Journalists' Syndicate membership on that basis. Journalists' Syndicate members refused to open their union to broadcasters, not least because of the weight of numbers at the ERTU and fears that this would increase the Syndicate's vulnerability to government manipulation. In a long-running controversy, the Journalists' Syndicate urged broadcast journalists to set up a union of their own, which they could not do without Ministry of Information backing. Two options were envisaged: a union especially for the ERTU or one for broadcast journalists generally.

The latter option was proposed to the wider media community at the end of March 2012, at a conference on broadcasting co-sponsored by BBC Arabic, Al-Ahram Regional Press Institute, and a nascent syndicate for *i'lamiyin* (media workers). Since the term *i'lamiyin* differs from the usual Arabic word for journalists (*sahafiyin*), which in turn is linked to the word for newspapers, it implied that the syndicate was intended primarily for broadcasters. Introducing it at the conference's opening session, the syndicate coordinator, Adel Noureddin, said that membership of the body would be open to any media person or specialist 'who cares about the future of audiovisual media in Egypt'. He stressed that it would bring people together regardless of their affiliations.[17] One month later, Noureddin won approval from the parliamentary Committee for Culture, Information and Tourism for a bill to establish the syndicate for broadcasters. But the bill, which still needed legal redrafting, became a casualty of the dissolution of Parliament.

Several waves of protest by those working at the ERTU's Maspero building in 2011-12, on behalf of better journalism, made it plain that media workers in the building needed protection from management reprisals against protestors. Channel 2 presenter Hala Helmy of the Media Revolutionaries group, one of those campaigning for radical change in the state broadcaster, said in October 2011 that the group was trying to organise defending the rights of anyone arbitrarily fired for 'bringing a certain guest or defying the order of the state security in covering an event'.[18] Their approach to unionisation envisaged independent national syndicates for different types of media work, such as television presenters or photographers. Journalists' Syndicate officials offered the use of Syndicate facilities to those trying to organise within the ERTU, but their support was primarily for a broadcasters' union. Secretary General and Vice Chair Abeer Saadi said:

> We encourage [broadcast journalists] to have their own syndicate. It should be their initiative. We opposed the creation of a second syndicate for print journalists but it would be OK to have another syndicate for people working in a different part of the media. We want to have two strong syndicates. Online journalists can join [the Journalists' Syndicate] after the laws are amended.[19]

Abeer Saadi was one of the officials elected in the Journalists' Syndicate's first free elections, held in October 2011. The elections were slightly delayed by a court battle over the legitimacy of the interim council that had overseen the forced resignation of Makram Mohammed Ahmad as chairman in February. But they finally went ahead on 26 October, with 103 nominees for the 12 council posts and three contenders for chairman. The results showed a close race. Saadi, head of training and professional development at the Syndicate for four years before her election as secretary general, won 1,659 votes. This was the most votes of any candidate, including Mamdouh el-Waly, deputy editor at *Al-Ahram*, who was elected chairman with 1,646 votes. Waly, who rejected the Muslim Brotherhood label that some wanted to attach to him, won by a margin of 247 votes over Yehia Qallash, of *Al-Gumhuriya*.

The election also brought in new blood, as only half those elected to the council were existing members. Among the re-elected was Mohamed Abdel-Quddous, head of the Freedoms Committee, the only member of the new council openly identified with the Muslim Brotherhood. In May 2012, after six employees from the Muslim Brotherhood's television channel Misr25 and 20 other journalists from newspapers including *Al-Badeel*, *Al-Watan*, *Al-Masry al-Youm*, and *Al-Tahrir* were assaulted while covering clashes in the Cairo district of Abbassiya, a Muslim Brotherhood website quoted Abdel-Quddous as warning that the Journalists' Syndicate was 'leaning towards' calling on its members to refrain from reporting SCAF news until all journalists detained during the clashes had been released.[20]

The effect of free and open elections was already evident in the Syndicate's actions vis-à-vis SCAF and the military prosecutor before May 2012. It lodged a formal complaint about military attacks on journalists soon after the elections and issued a statement on 16 November 2011 urging Egyptian journalists to register opposition to the practice of referring civilians to military courts. It thus became the first professional syndicate or trade union to speak out for civilians charged with offences to be tried by civilian judges, in accordance with the constitution,[21] and it stood by journalists who refused to respond to a summons from the military prosecutor.

After the composition of the first assembly to write Egypt's new constitution was revealed, on 25 March 2012, to be heavily Islamist, the Journalists' Syndicate decided not to take part in it. Mamdouh el-Waly was reportedly reluctant to withdraw, but did so on the grounds that the assembly failed to reflect the diversity of Egyptian society.[22] After Mohammed Morsi's election as president, however, Waly's alliance with the ruling Muslim Brotherhood emerged more strongly. When Morsi issued a declaration in November 2012, adding judicial powers to the executive and legislative powers he had already taken in August, the Journalists' Syndicate split between those threatening to strike in protest at the move and those, like Waly, who pronounced the threat to be invalid. As a member of the reconstituted Constituent Assembly, he also attended the late-night vote on the Draft Constitution in November 2012, disregarding a Syndicate Board decision to discipline any Syndicate member taking part in it.[23]

In the period before Morsi's election the Syndicate moved towards what the IFJ calls 'renovation' by thinking collectively about new models for media regulation that would focus on setting standards. In Egypt's case this involves rethinking the matrix of existing laws and regulations that control journalists' input into decisions on professional ethics. References to 'cleaning up the legal environment' are common in the speech of key Syndicate officials. Under the law that governs the Journalists' Syndicate and the Press Law, the Higher Press Council is the body that issues the Code of Ethics (*Mithaq al-Sharaf*, literally 'Covenant of Honour'), which the Syndicate's Board and General Assembly decide upon. During a 'Training Day' co-sponsored by UNESCO's Cairo Office at the Journalists Syndicate in April 2012, speakers from Indonesia, Pakistan, Germany, and Sweden shared their varied experience of regulatory bodies, ombudsmen, and attempts at self-regulation, all of them fundamentally at odds with Egypt's Higher Press Council.

According to Abeer Saadi, the day's deliberations were part of the Syndicate's determination to be 'proactive'. The Higher Press Council had been 'working against journalists', she said. 'If we are going to change that, we need to replace it with a new entity. We need to show that journalists are trying to change themselves.'[24] The examples of press councils chosen for discussion had various features of relevance to Egypt. The Indonesian Press Council was seen as a promising model because it has a supportive, not a punitive, role. Its primary purpose is to protect and develop press freedom,[25] which is not the same as protecting the press. It oversees the journalistic code of ethics and has authority to consider and resolve public complaints about press reports. Pakistan's Coalition for Ethical Journalism, formed in May 2012, provided a model – still under construction when its representative addressed the Journalists' Syndicate Cairo gathering in April – of collective support for professional ethics on the part of both organisations and individuals.

Voluntary codes at company level

In light of the legal logjam facing Egyptian journalists as they sought to forge new frameworks for professional links with each other across media sectors, some observers suggested that the most effective route to the long-term goal might be through the boardrooms, offices, and corridors of individual media corporations. A *Guide to Self-Regulation for Egyptian Media*, drafted under UNESCO auspices after discussions at the Journalists' Syndicate training day on press councils in April 2012, starts from a belief in developing a 'culture' of self-regulation. The training day produced a statement promising creation of a working group to continue 'concrete work' on setting up an independent body to adjudicate complaints related to journalism.[26] The *Guide*, however, notes that self-regulation is both internal and external. External self-regulation involves creating a national authority, such as a media council or commission, of the kind proposed both by the Journalists' Syndicate and the Morsi government, including Information Minister Abdel-Maqsoud. Internal self-regulation takes place inside individual companies.[27]

The *Guide*'s premise is that internal self-regulation can be achieved without setting up formal and rigid structures, since its basic requirement is a commitment to transparency, accountability, and responding promptly to public complaints, all of which are not only ethical but good for business, because they can 'help companies avoid costly legal disputes'. Commitment and moral courage, it states, are needed in the boardroom as well as among journalists. The behaviour of media owners and executives 'ultimately decides the quality of journalism ... Unless media are led by people of principle there is little chance that journalism will deliver the quality of information that communities need and democracy requires'.[28]

Globally, the number of media companies committing themselves to international codes on transparency is minute. The Amsterdam-based Global Reporting Initiative (GRI), a non-profit body that has developed a reporting framework aimed at promoting corporate social responsibility as well as economic and environmental sustainability, has 600 'organizational stakeholders' in 60 countries. Only 15 of these have anything to do with the media and only two (public relations companies) are in the media business.[29] The fact that there are no GRI stakeholder companies of any kind in Egypt reflects a history of government corruption and a lack of local incentives to provide information on corporate governance. A study of Egyptian public–private joint ventures, published in 2012, found that much greater levels of transparency and much more evidence of overall accountability were required for members of the public to be able to judge whether these ventures were complying with their legal, social, or environmental responsibilities.[30] In the rush to create new media outlets in 2011, mutating ownership arrangements were often so opaque that journalists had difficulty reporting on them, let alone their sense of mission.

Despite this, or perhaps because of it, Egypt was one of six countries chosen to be part of an Ethical Journalism Network programme, established in 2012, with the aim of strengthening good corporate governance through a commitment to internal transparency and self-regulation by owners as well as journalists and citizen media. The Ethical Journalism Network is partnered with several international bodies, including the International Press Institute and European Broadcasting Union, but its closest partner, in terms of shared facilities, is the Global Editors Network, itself a relatively new initiative that started life in March 2011 as a spin-off from the Paris-based World Editors Forum. By mid-2012, ten Egyptian executives were among the 600 members of the Global Editors Network. They represented a range of state-run and privately owned publications, including three from *Al-Ahram*, two from *Al-Gumhuriya*, two from *Al-Youm al-Sabea*, and one each from Horytna, Al-Masry Media Corporation (owner of *Al-Masry al-Youm*), and the Egypt Media Development Programme.

The Ethical Journalism Network seeks to bring these and other journalists, editors, and media owners together behind joint actions for 'new standards of media accountability'.[31] In practical terms this is taken to mean encouraging more professional cooperation across all forms of journalism online and offline, and establishing a 'Trust in Media' standard that would allow journalists and media, individually and collectively, to register support for minimum standards of ethics and transparency. By this means the network would equip itself to engage with Egypt's president and government on repeal of laws that 'currently cast a long shadow over how journalism is practised across all platforms of media'.[32]

Scope for cross-border support

Initiatives to set standards in journalism inevitably have a dual character. Periodic events such as workshops and conferences push an initiative or a network into the public eye. Behind these, however, is the daily toil of advocacy and lobbying work that gives meaning to the events. Under Egyptian law during the Mubarak era, the perceived political nature of human rights advocacy for freedom of expression and association left advocacy groups in a permanent state of insecurity. Law No. 84 of 2002 prohibited non-governmental organisations (NGOs) from engaging in political activities and restricted their access to foreign funding. In 2009, for example, after the Egyptian Organisation for Human Rights (EOHR) documented human rights abuses by the authorities in a number of reports, the minister of social solidarity threatened it with closure under Article 42 of Law 84/2002 for having received 'unauthorised' foreign funding.

Fears mounted in early 2012 that a new post-Mubarak law on NGOs would preserve these illiberal features. A draft from the Ministry of Social Solidarity even proposed closing the legal loophole whereby advocacy groups could register as companies. In May 2012 the EOHR commented negatively on a law drafted by the Human Rights Committee of the People's Assembly, which failed to recognise NGO work in the field of human rights and would have obliged NGOs to obtain official permission before accepting funds from any source, whether collective or individual, local, or foreign.[33] But fears about new legal provisions were ultimately sparked as much by actions as texts. In December 2011, after a crescendo of accusations that local NGOs were taking foreign funds illegally and using them to foment unrest, undermine Egypt's sovereignty, and divide the country, security forces raided 17 premises belonging to ten Egyptian and foreign civil society bodies. They took away money, documents, and computers and sealed the offices. In February 2012, criminal prosecutions were brought against 19 Americans and 24 Egyptians on counts of channelling funds illegally into political activities in Egypt.

One of the offices raided and closed was the newly established local branch of the Washington-based International Centre for Journalism (ICFJ). Its head, Yehia Ghanem, a journalist for 27 years, with experience as South Africa bureau chief for *Al-Ahram* and prizes for his war reporting from Bosnia and the Democratic Republic of Congo, was arrested. Other US pro-democracy groups affected attracted a great deal of attention, including the International Republican Institute, National Democratic Institute, and Freedom House. But the campaign was not only a backlash against a sudden surge in US spending in 2011 on training for all aspects of election campaigns. It also targeted Egyptian groups, including the Arab Centre for Independence of the Judiciary and the Legal Profession, and the Cairo office of Germany's Konrad Adenauer Foundation. The Cairo office head, Andreas Jacobs, who had reported in November 2011 on obstacles placed in the way of democratisation in Egypt, was called in for questioning.[34]

The debacle over NGO funding and activities calmed as 2012 progressed, but its repercussions continued to be felt at a personal and institutional level by many people involved in journalism projects, not least Yehia Ghanem. While most of the Americans indicted left Egypt, Ghanem and the ICFJ's office manager were among the Egyptians taken to court on charges that could bring prison sentences of five years. The state media, taking their lead from the international cooperation minister, Faiza Aboul-Naga, a Mubarak appointee who retained her position after his overthrow, published leaked court documents that appeared to accuse the groups of complicity with a US-Israeli plot.

The court case against the defendants, including Ghanem, was repeatedly postponed. First it was held over to April, then June and then July, when it was said that prosecution witnesses, including Aboul-Naga, would address the court behind closed doors.[35] In the end Aboul-Naga failed to show up, after the court reportedly excused her from appearing,[36] and the trial was postponed for a fifth and sixth time, and then, after some evidence was heard but closing statements were not concluded, adjourned to December. Aboul-Naga declined to serve in the cabinet sworn in at the beginning of August. Her replacement, Ashraf al-Arabi, a former chairman of the Egyptian Tax Authority, commended Aboul-Naga's 'strenuous and marvellous efforts during her time in office', but also stressed the importance of international cooperation during 'the coming phase'.³⁷ When the Shura Council announced a second round of new appointments to state-run publishing houses in September 2012, Yehia Ghanem was in the list as the new board chairman of Dar al-Helal.

Nevertheless, Ghanem's treatment during Aboul-Naga's tenure raised urgent issues of professional solidarity and press standards at *Al-Ahram*, whose deputy editor, Ahmad Moussa, had written an opinion piece introducing and approving the indictment text on 11 February 2012. A US think tank, the Project for Middle East Democracy, said the piece was an 'archetypal example of the state's tactics', being 'peppered with conspiratorial language' and published in 'a manner that colors the reader's interpretation of the charges'.³⁸ Ghanem complained that some colleagues at *Al-Ahram* had campaigned against him, without giving him the right to respond, and some had even called for him to be denied entry to the newspaper premises. But the board chairman said he should retain his title of deputy chief editor.³⁹

For others involved in advocacy relating to ethical journalism, the episode highlighted the urgency of resolving legal contradictions over freedom of association as well as those affecting freedom of expression. It demonstrated once again the difficulty of institutional capacity building for the media in authoritarian settings and showed why one-off training sessions are a considerably more attractive option for external bodies wanting to share their expertise with Egyptian journalists.⁴⁰ Yet Egyptian human rights advocates believe that training is not a priority activity for external involvement in journalism development in the country's post-Mubarak evolution. When US NGOs met with media law experts in June 2011 to discuss prospects for media development in Egypt and Tunisia, Egyptian human rights lawyer Negad al-Borei told them: 'Don't waste money on training. The problem is not a lack of information or qualifications but the difficulty of building economically viable institutions.'⁴¹

Borei, who was later on the defence team for NGOs accused of illegal activities, told the meeting that it was important to build up local radio and newspapers. There could be a radio station in every town, he said: for example, 'Esna radio, Luxor radio. Why not Saut Damanhour [Voice of Damanhour]? It's very cheap and will not take much effort and you will find many people who love to talk by that medium.' Newspapers in the provincial governorates have very low circulation, which makes them vulnerable to advertisers' demands, Borei continued. So why not support someone to work as an intern every day for six months with the management of a local newspaper in Gharbia, for example, so that it could become a 'real institution'. After that support could continue through Skype.[42]

Others point to the accelerating penetration of mobile internet in Egypt and the related shift in platforms for instant delivery of media content, suggesting that external support can help content providers build capacity to keep up with the shift. *Al-Masry al-Youm*, Horytna, and 25TV all took up this kind of help from Scandinavian sources. In readiness for covering parliamentary elections in 2011, staff from *Al-Masry al-Youm* acquired a mobile phone application that allows photos, sound, footage, and text to be packaged and sent in one file to speed reporting. The same paper was also part of the 'Checkdesk' project, to develop a digital platform for sorting, translating, and disseminating citizen media with the aim of improving trust between citizen journalists and professional journalists. Horytna journalists learned in 2010 how to use the Hindenburg Systems community radio editing tools to facilitate recording of sounds, atmosphere, and interviews in the street. 25TV won six months' support during the second half of 2012 to develop creative ideas and improve its administrative structure.

Another focus for capacity building has been investigative journalism. By mid-2012 the boards of no fewer than four privately owned Egyptian newspapers had responded to growing competition in their sector by setting up in-house investigation units with expertise in relevant legal issues, computer-assisted reporting, data management, and ensuring that stories are viable and fully checked and resourced. They did this in collaboration with Arab Reporters for Investigative Journalism (ARIJ), based in Amman, Jordan, which was also able to step up its material support to Egyptian newspapers to facilitate actual investigations in 2011–12. ARIJ, launched in 2006, had hitherto seen relatively timid efforts from Egypt, more in the nature of features than investigations.

Al-Masry al-Youm was the first to create a special unit in 2011. It investigated the dealings of Mubarak associate Hussein Salem, who stood accused of making billions from the sale of underpriced gas to Israel. But it also took on health and safety issues. Two of its reporters, Mohammed Al-Khuly and Ali Zalat, spent three days inside a dyeing plant in Shubra al-Kheima, using audio and video, partly under cover, for an investigation into the use of imported dyes. They researched European bans on certain dyeing substances, arranged chemical tests on textiles dyed locally, and documented health hazards to workers in unregulated dyeing plants. Their report, 'Carcinogenic clothes fill Egyptian markets', published in *Al-Masry al-Youm* on 13 June 2012, was completed with technical and financial help from ARIJ, under the supervision of Egyptian journalist Amr el-Kahky, Cairo bureau chief for Al-Jazeera English. The investigation prompted the Egyptian Organisation for Standards and Quality to tighten up its controls in line with those imposed in Europe and the USA.[43]

Al-Youm al-Sabea editor Khaled Saleh said his reason for setting up an investigations unit with help from ARIJ lay in the pressures of transforming the newspaper from a weekly to a daily in 2011. He told International Media Support, the Danish group that helps to fund ARIJ, that he saw investigative content as a way of differentiating the paper's print edition from its website and securing a loyal readership. 'If you follow a code of respecting readers and providing accurate information, then that is the newspaper that will last a long time', Saleh said.[44] *Al-Youm al-Sabea* had previously played a part in exposing police brutality and interior ministry lies about the killing of Khaled Said in Alexandria in June 2010, through the investigative reporting of Bahaa El-Taweel. Taweel later joined ONTV, where he became producer of Yosri Fouda's talkshow *Akher Kalam*. An investigation on the smuggling of banned pesticides into Egypt, written by Kamal Murad of *Al-Youm al-Sabea* under the supervision of Amr el-Kahky on behalf of ARIJ, reportedly took 18 months.

Al-Shorouk's investigations unit came into being in early 2012 as part of the paper's development strategy for 2011–14, after several of its journalists had attended ARIJ workshops, led by Egyptian trainers. *Al-Watan* quickly followed suit, just as it was about to hit the news-stands in April 2012. By September 2012, *Al-Watan* journalists had published investigations into hospitals and banks. In one they revealed how shortages of equipment and specialists at state-run hospitals were affecting the survival of premature babies. In another they exposed sharp practice on the part of banks that were taking advantage of lax government oversight at the expense of customers.

Labour and NGO laws' impact on free speech

The sharing of skills and the prominence of Egyptians among ARIJ affiliates is evidence that Egypt today has its own strong pool of experienced journalists, several with international reputations, who have first-hand experience of the situations their trainees are liable to face. What they and others say they want from international partners is sustained moral and technical support and legal aid for journalists targeted by vindictive security forces and penalised by repressive laws. These laws not only constrain media organisations and the content they produce but reach into the workplace, where, by limiting the opportunities for media practitioners to choose how best to represent their own interests and restricting media freedom advocacy groups from operating freely, they have an impact on the development of journalists' professional norms and practice.

In the months after President Morsi formed his government, prospects for radical change of the laws on unionisation and NGOs began to fade. In October 2012 the Ministry of Insurance and Social Affairs drafted a new law for regulating NGOs that still required them to obtain government permission before accepting foreign funding. The draft law set penalties of a year in jail and/or a £E 100,000 ($16,400) fine for anyone working with a foreign NGO in Egypt without government permission, or conducting surveys or field research without government permission.[45] The same month, responding to fears that Morsi's labour minister, Khaled al-Azhary, was seeking only cosmetic changes to the despised Trade Union Law of 1970, the two largest independent workers' groups, EFITU and the EDLC, together with like-minded political parties, formed an alliance to campaign for a law on trade union freedom that would guarantee workers' rights to free association and protect them against punitive dismissal.[46]

Confrontations over wide-ranging legal reforms were set to remain unresolved pending national agreement on a new constitution, eventual surrender of the wide-ranging powers assumed by the President in 2012, and elections to a new Parliament. But, as this chapter has argued, future prospects for wholesale legal reform are nonetheless central to the situation of journalists, just as an awareness of the legal and political background is central to an understanding of contemporary Egyptian journalism. As noted by Reem Abou-El-Fadl, an Oxford University scholar of international relations who writes regularly for the Egyptian press, the 'most effective international practitioners are those with knowledge of the historical context'.[47] Made in relation to the concept of transitional justice and its applicability to Egypt, Abou-El-Fadl's point about knowledge is also valid for other fields. Egyptian rights activists are aiming at far-reaching goals. Their aspirations also call for a transformation in how people abroad perceive and respond to their situation.

5

Conclusions

Any worthwhile observations to be made about recent transformations in Egyptian journalism need to be prefaced with a word about history. This is not just a necessary antidote to the preoccupation with the here-and-now of social media and citizen journalism that tended to dominate early commentary on the revolutionary uprising of January 2011. As Chapters 2 and 3 of this book have shown, present-day idiosyncrasies of journalism in Egypt owe a great deal to historically specific structures created by state media monopolies under Nasser and by the partial, mostly false, liberalisation measures taken under Sadat and Mubarak.

They also reflect a tradition of resistance to those structures on the part of a significant number of Egyptian journalists, including those who honed their skills in Gulf-based pan-Arab print and broadcast media because of the inhospitable climate at home. Today, many long-suppressed rifts between opposing traditions are in the open: over some journalists' closeness to state security operations; over the right place for opinion and editorialising; over lines of accountability and whether they flow upward to the ruling power or outward to the public; over journalists' obligations in terms of accuracy and correcting errors; over the best models of professional representation for journalists. Having deepened over decades the rifts will not be quick to heal.

That said, the seven years from 2005 to 2012 saw a particularly rapid transformation in styles and uses of journalism, which helped to expose the rifts as a prelude to resolving them. One major catalyst was the strength of opposition among diverse socio-political forces in 2004–5 to yet another plebiscite for a dictator and his dynastic ambitions. These forces found an outlet in new media spaces, where they could challenge government corruption, election rigging, police brutality, and unemployment. Journalists working in new genres of newspaper and television talkshow interacted with bloggers and activists using Facebook and Twitter. In the process, reporters who valued objectivity found themselves boxed into a stereotype of anti-government activist, simply because there was so little relevant news to report that put the government in a favourable, or even neutral, light. With a fresh round of innovation in media outlets and news-gathering activity after January 2011, practitioners struggled to define the different but overlapping codes and rationales of activism, citizen journalism, and professional journalism.

In the aftermath of Mubarak's overthrow, lines between journalism and activism were blurred by the struggle to report effectively on the military's repeated use of lethal force against continuing protests in major cities. Given demand for footage that was both timely and credible, mainstream media could rely on social media and video-sharing sites, or they could send their own reporters to the scene. One new television venture hired young trainees from among the activists, giving them a remit to engage in participatory networks and integrate social media with other sources. Other print and broadcasting outlets reinforced their social media desks. The challenge of integration sparked innovative journalistic activity – described by its practitioners as a 'new kind of journalism' – in the form of the Mosireen collective's proactive gathering and verification of footage, and its dissemination through street screenings organised by the activist group Kazeboon. Demand for authenticity was the common thread between trusted offline journalists and online activists; insistence on balanced coverage was where they differed.

As the integration of online and offline sources advanced, it accentuated an alternative dividing line – between so-called journalists, who stayed in their offices to reproduce first the generals' and then the Muslim Brotherhood's versions of events, and the expanding spectrum of reporters who braved bullets and intimidation to gather news. These lines were by no means neatly drawn between government-run media on the one hand and everyone else. In almost monthly bouts of violence between October 2011 and May 2012, fewer state-employed journalists were reported injured than those from privately owned or community media. But, contrary to the impression given by headlines in government-controlled media, a significant number of state-employed journalists, many of whom had already revolted during the initial 18-day uprising when an *Al-Ahram* colleague was fatally shot, held protracted demonstrations in their workplaces and joined protests at the Journalists' Syndicate, demanding guarantees of safety, editorial autonomy, and overhaul of their newsrooms.

Although state-run media bodies remained untransformed in terms of their management and structures, their tens of thousands of employees split irreconcilably. On the one hand were small active groups keen to articulate revolutionary expectations, including new ownership and organisational models for the ERTU, Al-Ahram Press Organisation, and other publications. On the other hand were the much larger groups of time-servers, recruited through Mubarak-era nepotism, with a vested interest in the status quo. Media monitoring revealed some degree of change in state media news coverage, with more attention finally paid to Egypt's regions in contrast to the Cairo-centric focus of the past. The ERTU's long-neglected regional channels received help in preparing for election coverage and one of them co-produced a version of the BBC's *Question Time* format in Upper Egypt, which demonstrated citizens' appetite for holding local politicians to account.

Voices speaking up for a public service ethos were heard as much outside state media as inside them, testifying to journalists' interest in operational models that would communicate 'from the people to the people' and shield editorial coverage from business as well as government pressures. As owners from the Mubarak era reasserted control over privately owned print and broadcast media, journalists in these media discovered they still could not count on their employers to support professionalism and free speech. Lacking permission to raise capital from ordinary citizens through the stock market, and held back by an unreconstructed advertising industry still working to Mubarak era norms, journalists' public service media initiatives faced an uphill struggle. In these circumstances, Egyptian advocates of raising journalism standards urged international donors to prioritise capacity building and legal aid over the one-off training sessions previously favoured by some donors, which local journalists are well able to provide.

The unprecedented physical attacks on so many reporters helped to galvanise organisational activity among journalists, which came up against Egypt's failure to meet its international commitments to allow freedom of association. As with so many other areas of legal reform, the possibilities for resolving contradictions in favour of pluralism were frozen in June 2012 when the elected Parliament was dissolved. With SCAF continuing to resist civilian oversight, the new civilian president taking legislative power to himself and defying the judiciary, and the ruling party stuffing state-run media houses with its own appointees, the environment for Egyptian journalism nearly two years after the revolutionary uprising looked little different from what went before. Yet, as emerges from evidence presented here, changes in many areas of journalism practice were too fundamental to be undone.

Recommendations

Recommendations implicit in this study's findings are in line with many made by Egyptian media freedom advocacy groups. First, the future of the country's new constitution is central to any recommendations about journalism, since it should underpin safeguards for freedom of expression and association and limit the government's power to restrict either. Constitutional change should feed into media law reform, so that legal provisions are not only brought into line with Egypt's commitments under international human rights conventions, but also allow for the full range of media types, including community media, that exist in the digitally converged environment. The Penal Code should be amended to remove rules that criminalise journalistic work deemed 'insulting' to public officials. Amending the laws on defamation would, among other things, help to promote good practice in cross-media participatory reporting that draws on blogs and social media for the purpose of increasing transparency about public affairs. There is an urgent need to separate the public broadcaster from the information ministry and end the system whereby the ruling party, through the upper house of Parliament, appoints editors in publicly owned print media.

Journalists employed by the enormous broadcasting and press bodies that have been controlled by government for the last half century will not be free to practise ethically and professionally unless these bodies are divided into more manageable units, made independent, and their managements thoroughly overhauled. The financial regulator should not block mechanisms, which have been proposed, to achieve direct public ownership of the media through initial public offerings and the trading of shares on the stock market, provided measures are in place to prevent ownership concentration. Independence should go hand-in-hand with decentralisation, so that Egypt's long-neglected regions can develop their own journalism and bring regional news regularly to a national audience.

Journalists should avail themselves of their right under international law to form any representative or other professional body they choose without needing an Act of Parliament or other permission to do so. Concerns about union fragmentation can be overcome through an umbrella federation. There is a need for public acknowledgement that good journalism is not possible in corrupt environments. Owners, editors, and journalists should take advantage of current initiatives to agree cross-platform ethical standards that will underpin corporate transparency and accountability to media users, which is needed to gain public trust. Journalists and their employers should be encouraged to be active members in global networks and international membership bodies, such as associations of broadcasters, regulators, newspaper ombudsmen, and senior editors, whose membership criteria promote good practice.

Finally, donor countries and donor NGOs should follow the example of those bodies that have pledged help to build capacity of media institutions. In part this involves working in non-editorial departments to secure revenue streams that will buttress editorial independence. Where journalism is concerned it means providing legal aid, support for investigative work, and help with tools for adapting reporting techniques in line with shifts in modes of media consumption.

Notes

Chapter 1   A National Rethink of News Values

1. Quoted by Bel Trew in 'Egypt Citizen Journalism "Mosireen" Tops YouTube', *AhramOnline*, 20 Jan. 2012: http://english.ahram.org.eg/News/32185.aspx.
2. http://www.youtube.com/watch?v=ZWsszj2OBvQ.
3. Salah Abdel Maqsoud, 'Egypt's Media Revolution', *Guardian*, 15 Feb. 2011.
4. AFP, 'Egypt's Shamed State Media Squirms in New Era', 14 Feb. 2011.
5. Lina El-Wardani, *AhramOnline*, 27 Jan. 2011: http://english.ahram.org.eg/NewsContent/1/64/4914/Egypt/Politics-/Reporters-first-hand-account-of-Egypt-police-bruta.aspx.
6. http://english.ahram.org.eg/NewsContent/1/64/5134/Egypt/Politics-/Egypt-Symbolic-funeral-of-journalist-killed-by-pol.aspx.
7. Reuters, 'Egypt State Media Change Tune After Mubarak's Fall', 16 Feb. 2011.
8. Reporters sans Frontières, *Press Freedom Index* (2011/12): http://en.rsf.org/spip.php?page=classement&id_rubrique=1043.
9. Reporters sans Frontières, *Upheaval in the Arab World* (Nov. 2011), 6.
10. Jack Shenker, 'Egypt's Revolution Won't End with the Presidential Election', guardian.co.uk, 23 May 2012: http://www.guardian.co.uk/commentisfree/2012/may/23/egypt-revolution-presidential-election.
11. http://www.jadaliyya.com/pages/index/3642/a-year-in-the-life-of-egypts-media_a-2011-timeline; http://weekly.ahram.org.eg/2012/1082/sc24.htm.
12. Abdel-Rahman Hussein, *Egypt Independent*, 11 July 2011: http://www.egyptindependent.com/news/24-january-op-ed-new-information-minister-expressed-concern-about-uprising.
13. The news ticker on http://www.youtube.com/watch?v=8h8LRoF3tFM&feature=related reads 'One dead and 20 injured after Coptic protestors open fire on them at Maspero'.
14. http://www.ebu.ch/en/union/news/2011/tcm_6-72864.php?display=EN.
15. http://eipr.org/en/press release/2011/11/22/1288.
16. Law No. 34 of 2011.
17. *Mubasher* means 'direct', *Misr* means Egypt.
18. The title means 'Our country in Egyptian [i.e. Egyptian dialect of Arabic]'.
19. *Egypt Independent*, 29 Oct. 2011: http://www.egyptindependent.com/news/journalist-summoned-military-prosecutor.

NOTES TO PAGES 8-13

20 Amnesty International UK, 'Jailed Egyptian Blogger is a Prisoner of Conscience', 14 Dec. 2011: http://www.amnesty.org.uk/news_details.asp?NewsID=19861.
21 Al-Masry Al-Youm staff, *Egypt Independent*, 9 Oct. 2011: http://www.egyptindependent.com/news/live-updates-death-toll-rises-clashes-mobs-attack-christian-businesses.
22 CPJ alert, New York, 21 Nov. 2011.
23 Salma Shukrallah, *AhramOnline*, 19 Dec. 2011: http://english.ahram.org.eg/NewsContentPrint/1/0/29717/Egypt/0/Journalists-targeted-for-exposing-Egypt-stateviol.aspx.
24 See the full list of injuries at http://cpj.org/2011/12/egypt-must-investigate-attacks-on-the-press.php. They include the high-profile case of Egyptian-American Mona Eltahawy.
25 *AhramOnline*, 22 Dec. 2011: http://english.ahram.org.eg/NewsContent/1/64/29976/Egypt/Politics-/Cabinet-crackdown-leaves--dead,--injured-.aspx.
26 http://cpj.org/2011/12/in-egypt-press-freedom-abuses-must-be-investigated.php.
27 Ali Abdel-Mohsen, *Egypt Independent*, 19 Dec. 2011: http://www.egyptindependent.com/news/mondays-papers-question-marks.
28 http://www.filfan.com/News.asp?newsid=23740; http://www.filfan.com/News.asp?newsid=23743.
29 A text translation of the Mosireen video is available at http://www.jadaliyya.com/pages/index/3599/ghadas-testimony-on-being-tortured-by-the-egyptian.
30 Ali Abdel-Mohsen, *Egypt Independent*, 19 Dec. 2011: http://www.egyptindependent.com/news/mondays-papers-question-marks.
31 *Egypt Independent*, 19 Dec. 2011: http://www.egyptindependent.com/news/politicians-criticize-hitler-statements-made-army-official.
32 Dahlia Kholaif, 10 June 2012: http://www.bloomberg.com/news/2012-06-10/egyptian-television-stops-ad-portraying-foreigners-as-spies.html.
33 Eman al-Shenawi, 'Egypt's "Anti-Tahrir" Ad Seen as "Smear Campaign"', 18 June 2012: http://www.alarabiya.net/articles/2012/06/18/221340.html.
34 Shotgun pellets may be large ('buckshot') or small ('birdshot'). Reports of eye and other injuries in Egyptian demonstrations indicate use of both. Use of birdshot against protestors in Bahrain has been blamed for a number of deaths.
35 http://www.youtube.com/watch?v=7JhA4jIv4bk.
36 See Freedom and Justice Party website, 7 May 2012: http://fjponline.com/article.php?id=688.
37 In the translation published by Reuters, Okasha had said in a talk show that Morsi and his group 'deserved to get killed' and *El-Destour* had accused the Muslim Brotherhood of 'leading Egypt to its worst decades ... filled with killing and bloodshed'. See Yasmine Saleh, 'Egypt's Mursi Accused of Stifling Dissent in Media Crackdown', Reuters, 17 Aug. 2012.
38 Quoted by Shahira Amin in 'Egypt's Media Revolution Only Beginning', *Index on Censorship*, 17 Jan. 2012: http://uncut.indexoncensorship.org/2012/01/egypt-media-revolution.
39 Military interests are estimated to hold up to 40 per cent of the Egyptian economy. In Mubarak's time, US diplomats in Cairo saw these holdings as the reason for military opposition to economic reform. See Shana Marshall and Joshua Stacher,

'Egypt's Generals and Transnational Capital', *Middle East Report*, 262 (Spring 2012): http://www.merip.org/mer/mer262/egypts-generals-transnational-capital.
40 http://egyptianchronicles.blogspot.co.uk/2011/03/unforgettable-night-in-arab-tv-history.htm.
41 'Ya' is put before a name to attract attention, or make clear that someone is being addressed directly.
42 Roula Khalaf and Heba Saleh, 'Egypt's Generals Squirm under Grilling', *Financial Times*, 20 Oct. 2011.
43 http://www.arabawy.org/tag/storming-ss-nasr-city.
44 The page had 473,000 users at the time, according to Jennifer Preston, *New York Times*, 5 Feb. 2011. Shazli said her team had hunted high and low for Ghoneim in the city's police stations and hospitals. English subtitles are available at http://www.guardian.co.uk/world/video/2011/feb/08/egypt-activist-wael-ghonim-google-video.
45 Amr Salama, quoted by H.J. Cummins, 'ICFJ Training Leads to Top-Ranked News Source in "Arab Spring"': http://anywhere.icfj.atendesigngroup.com/impact-stories/347.
46 According to filmmaker Tamer Said, speaking to the author, Cairo, 26 Jan. 2012, and Lubna Darwish and Omar Robert Hamilton, quoted by Bel Trew, in 'Egypt Citizen Journalism "Mosireen" Tops YouTube', *AhramOnline*, 20 Jan. 2012: http://english.ahram.org.eg/News/32185.aspx.
47 According to Eissa's partner, Ahmad Abu Haiba, speaking to the author, Budapest, 25 June 2011.
48 For example, TV preacher Amr Khaled's programme *Words from the Heart*, Prince Alwaleed bin Talal's Risalah channel, and Abu Haiba's own music channel 4Shabab.
49 Amir Makar, '25TV editors on Resuming Broadcast After Security Raid', *Daily News Egypt*, 13 Nov. 2011.
50 Results from different sources are collated at the Thomson Reuters Foundation website *Aswat Masriya* (Egyptian Voices): http://en.aswatmasriya.com/news/view.aspx?id=d4171c22-ef58-4c66-b0fa-c53df5ec38ef.

Chapter 2   Lessons from the Push for Professional Autonomy

1 For example, Larry Diamond, 'Thinking about Hybrid Regimes', *Journal of Democracy*, 13/2 (Apr. 2002), 31. Diamond, who also used the term 'pseudo-democracy', categorised Egypt as 'hegemonic electoral authoritarian' because of its uncompetitive elections.
2 Reda Helal, a senior editor at *Al-Ahram*, disappeared in Aug. 2003 and the outcome of the official investigation was never revealed. In Nov. 2004, Abdel-Halim Qandil, editor of *Al-Karama*, was abducted at knifepoint, beaten, and dumped in the desert without clothes.
3 See Maye Kassem's analysis in *Egyptian Politics: The Dynamics of Authoritarian Rule* (Lynne Rienner Publishers, 2004), 37-8.
4 Robert Springborg, 'Protest Against a Hybrid State: Words without Meaning?', in Nicholas Hopkins (ed.), *Political and Social Protest in Egypt*, themed issue of *Cairo Papers in Social Science*, 29/2-3 (2009), 7. Springborg is the US academic whose Dec. 2011 article on SCAF for *Egypt Independent* was censored (see Ch. 1).

NOTES TO PAGES 22–27

5 Springborg, 'Protest Against a Hybrid State', 16–17.
6 See, for example, Rabab El-Mahdi and Philip Marfleet (eds), *Egypt: Moment of Change* (AUC Press, 2009); Asef Bayat, *Life as Politics: How Ordinary People Change the Middle East* (AUC Press, 2009); and Bahgat Korany (ed.), *The Changing Middle East* (AUC Press, 2010).
7 http://baheyya.blogspot.co.uk/2007/09/death-of-deference.html, 16 Sept. 2007. For a detailed study of the 'tame fare', see Yorck von Korff, *Missing the Wave: Egyptian Journalists' Contribution to Democratization in the 1990s* (Deutsches Orient-Institut, 2003).
8 'Deep state' refers to a coalition of anti-democratic forces controlling politics behind the formalities of civilian rule. Issandr El Amrani, 'Sightings of the Egyptian Deep State', *Middle East Report Online*, 1 Jan. 2012: http://www.merip.org/mero/mero010112.
9 Translation from http://www.democracy-reporting.org/files/egypt_draft_constitution_unofficial_translation_dri.pdf.
10 Daniel Hallin and Paolo Mancini, *Comparing Media Systems* (Cambridge University Press, 2004), 34–5.
11 Arthur Goldschmidt, *A Biographical Dictionary of Modern Egypt* (Lynne Rienner Publishers, 2000), 6.
12 Adel Darwish, 'Obituary: Mustafa Amin', *Independent*, 15 Apr. 1997.
13 See the list in Sonia Dabous, 'Nasser and the Egyptian Press', in Charles Tripp (ed.), *Contemporary Egypt: Through Egyptian Eyes* (Routledge, 1993), 108.
14 See, for example, Reem Saad, 'Shame, Reputation and Egypt's Lovers: A Controversy over the Nation's Image', *Visual Anthropology*, 10/2–4 (1998), 401–12.
15 Jeffrey Black, 'Egypt's Press: More Free, Still Fettered', *Arab Media and Society* (Jan. 2008): www.arabmediasociety.org/?article=572, p. 8.
16 Maurice Chammah, 'The Scene of the Crime: October 9th, Maspero, and Egyptian Journalism After the Revolution', *Arab Media and Society*, 15 (Spring 2012): http://www.arabmediasociety.com/?article=783.
17 Ibid.
18 Colin Sparks, 'Media and Transition in Latin America', *Westminster Papers in Communication and Culture*, 8/1 (June 2011), 11.
19 Augusto Valeriani, 'Pan-Arab Satellite Television and Arab National Information Systems: Journalists' Perspectives on a Complicated Relationship', *Middle East Journal of Culture and Communication*, 3/1 (2010), 26–42.
20 See the revealing quotations, ibid. 34.
21 According to Al-Jazeera Programme Director Aref Hijjawi, in 'The Role of Al-Jazeera (Arabic) in the Arab Revolts of 2011', *Perspectives* (Heinrich Böll Stiftung), 2 (May 2011), 70.
22 Interview with Sajini Dularamani, *Al-Ahram Weekly*, 15–21 Apr. 1999: http://weekly.ahram.org.eg/1999/425/profile.htm.
23 Interview with Andrew Hammond in Nov. 2001, quoted in Hammond's *Popular Culture in the Arab World* (AUC Press, 2007), 219.
24 See Mansour's comments in Ahmad Osman, 'Rude Awakening: Dream Drops Top Talkers', *Transnational Broadcasting Studies*, 12 (Spring/Summer 2004): http://www.tbsjournal.com/Archives/Spring04/dream.htm.

25 Bradley Hope, 'Egypt's "Oprah" Returns to Television', *The National*, 24 Aug. 2011.
26 Shaden Shehab, 'Devil in the Detail', *Al-Ahram Weekly*, 833 (22–28 Feb. 2007).
27 Youssef Rakha, 'Hafez Marazi: Arab Contemporary', *Al-Ahram Weekly*, 805 (27 July–2 Aug. 2006).
28 *Variety* correspondent Ali Jaafar summarised the point from Mirazi's *Al-Hayat* interview in a piece on 6 July 2007: http://www.variety.com/article/VR1117968160?refcatid=2523.
29 Author's interview, Cairo, 3 Aug. 2011.
30 Arabic transcript of the 4 Dec. 2006 episode of *Min Washington*, downloaded from Al-Jazeera's online archives on 12 Aug. 2011.
31 Lamia Hassan, 'On the Clock: Moataz El-Demerdash', *Egypt Today* (Oct. 2010), 49.
32 Emad Mekay, 'Report on Latest from Cairo', 26 Jan. 2011, Institute for Public Accuracy: http://www.accuracy.org/report-on-latest-from-cairo.
33 The 28 Jan. 2011 edition of the *Egyptian Gazette Online* carried an account of the calls.
34 Quoted by Ramadan Kader, 'A Show of Anger', *Egyptian Gazette*, 28 May 2012.
35 Author's interview, Cairo, 1 Aug. 2011.
36 As reported from Cairo by Dubai-based *Gulf News*, 10 Nov. 2009.
37 Author's interview with *Al-Qahira al-youm* production staff, Cairo, 1 Aug. 2011.
38 Adel Iskander included a link to a copy of the memo in his second entry for 31 Dec. 2011 at http://www.jadaliyya.com/pages/index/3642/a-year-in-the-life-of-egypts-media_a-2011-timeline.
39 See Joshua Muravchik's account in *The Next Founders: Voices of Democracy in the Middle East* (National Book Network, 2009), 171–2.
40 Quoted by Magdi Samaan, 'ONTV Kicks Off', *Daily News Egypt*, 7 Oct. 2008.
41 Conversation with the author, London, 12 May 2008.
42 Shaden Shehab, 'Paper Trails', *Al-Ahram Weekly*, 1019 (14–20 Oct. 2010).
43 *Daily News Egypt*, 6 Oct. 2010.
44 *Al-Ahram Weekly*, 1013 (26 Aug.–1 Sept. 2010).
45 Author's interview with Hafez al-Mirazi, Cairo, 3 Aug. 2011.
46 Ibid.
47 http://www.charlierose.com/view/interview/11472.
48 Both Rateb and Bahgat were quoted by Noha Hennawy, 27 Sept. 2010: http://www.egyptindependent.com/news/tv-show-bans-prompt-fears-pre-election-crackdown-private-media.
49 Rowainy accused protestors of being armed and boasted that he had been able to control the mood in Tahrir Square immediately before 11 Feb. See *Daily News Egypt*, 'TV Hostess Sacked over Defending Columnist's Integrity', 24 July 2011.
50 Quoted by several sources, including Manar Ammar at the online news website http://bikyamasr.com/37306/egypt-tv-host-axed-over-interviewing-military-official.
51 Sherif Awad, 'Straight Talk: Dina Abdel-Rahman on Being Off the Air', *Egypt Today*, May 2012.
52 Ibid.
53 Ibid.
54 *Al-Ashera Masa'an*, 22 Feb. 2011.
55 Author's interview, Cairo, 3 Aug. 2011.

56 Author's interview, London, 10 Jan. 2012.
57 Hugh Miles, *Al-Jazeera: How Arab TV News Challenged the World* (Abacus, 2005), 183. In 2009, Fouda appended the full four-line passage after his sign-off on email circulars.
58 There are tiny variations in the translation depending on the source; for example, *Al-Akhbar* English version, 22 Oct. 2011: http://english.al-akhbar.com/node/1129; *Daily News Egypt*, 10 Nov. 2011.
59 BBC *HardTalk* interview with Stephen Sackur, 1 Nov. 2011: http://www.bbc.co.uk/iplayer/episode/b016pqh0/HARDtalk_Yosri_Fouda_Egyptian_journalist.
60 Conversation with the author, Cairo, 23 Jan. 2012.
61 Ekram Ibrahim, *AhramOnline*, 17 May 2012: http://english.ahram.org.eg/NewsContent/1/64/41905/Egypt/Politics-/Yosri-Fouda-to-quit-Egyptian-TV.aspx.
62 *AhramOnline*, 21 July 2012: http://english.ahram.org.eg/NewsContent/1/64/45748/Egypt/Politics-/ONTVs-Yosri-Fouda-suspends-Egypt-show-over-alleged.aspx.
63 Quoted by *Egypt Independent*, 21 June 2012: http://www.egyptindependent.com/news/yosri-fouda-halt-production-talk-show-out-respect.
64 Information and Decision Support Centre, quoted by *Daily News Egypt*, 31 July 2008.
65 Safaa Abdoun, 'The Power of Facebook Takes New Shape in 2008', *Daily News Egypt*, 23 Dec. 2008.
66 http://www.socialbakers.com/facebook-statistics/egypt.
67 Interviewed by Sami Ben Gharbia, 30 Apr. 2008, for *Global Voices Online*: http://globalvoicesonline.org/2008/04/30/egypt-facebooking-the-struggle.
68 Heba Saleh et al., 'Arab Dissent Finds Voice in Cyberspace', *Financial Times*, 2 July 2009.
69 Dubai School of Government, *Arab Social Media Report* (May 2011), 16.
70 Hana Zubair, 'Shahira Amin', *Egypt Today* (Jan. 2012), 55.
71 Lawrence Pintak and Yosri Fouda, 'Blogging in the Middle East: Not Necessarily Journalistic', 17 Aug. 2009: http://www.cjr.org/behind_the_news/the_new_threat_to_middle_east.php?page=all.
72 Ibid.
73 See pp. 112–13 of Mark Deuze, 'The Professional Identity of Journalists in the Context of Convergence Culture', *Observatorio Journal*, 7 (2008), 103–17.
74 Author's interview, Cairo, 23 Jan. 2012.
75 BBC *HardTalk* interview, see n. 59.
76 Interviewed by Passant Rabie for 'Mosireen: From Ground Zero', *Egypt Today*, Mar. 2012.
77 Linda Herrera, 12 Feb. 2011: http://www.jadaliyya.com/pages/index/612/egypts-revolution-2.0_the-facebook-factor.
78 Ibid.
79 Mohammad Al Abdallah, International Journalists' Network, 1 Sept. 2011: http://ijnet.org/stories/ten-tips-citizen-journalists-cairos-tweet-nadwa.
80 Zeinab al-Gundy, *AhramOnline*, 30 Jan. 2012: http://english.ahram.org.eg/NewsContent/1/114/32610/Egypt/-January-Revolution-continues/Twitters-role-in-revolutionary-Egypt--isolation-or.aspx.
81 Quoted by Ahmad Kotb, 'Money into Air? Investing in Egypt's Media', 9 Sept. 2011: http://english.ahram.org.eg/NewsContent/3/12/20187/Business/Economy/Money-into-air--investing-in-Egypts-media.aspx.

82. Daria Solovieva, 'Revolutionary Take on Broadcast Media', *Business Today*, Dec. 2011.
83. Deuze, 'Professional Identity', 113.
84. Ibid., 109.
85. *Egypt Human Development Report 2010* (UNDP and Egypt National Institute of Planning, 2010), 151. The jobless rate measures how many of the not-in-school population are unemployed or inactive.
86. Hossam Hamalawy, quoted by Zeinab al-Gundy, 30 Jan. 2012, see n. 80.
87. Fathy Abou Hatab, quoted by Stephanie Rice and Reem Abdel-Latif, 'Egyptian Press Still Not Free', *globalpost.com*, 21 Nov. 2011: http://www.globalpost.com/dispatch/news/regions/middle-east/egypt/111121/egyptian-press-still-not-free.
88. Quoted by *Variety Arabia*, 10 May 2012: http://varietyarabia.com/Docs.Viewer/4ffd8387-5826-4db7-a13d-e20763dd7cd0/default.aspx.
89. Quoted by *Enigma Magazine*, 'On Top with ONTV', 5 Sept. 2011: http://www.enigma-mag.com/interview_archives/2011/09/albert-shafik-august-2011.

Chapter 3 Stimuli for a Public Service Ethos

1. For an abundance of detail on this process, see Eberhard Kienle, *A Grand Delusion: Democracy and Economic Reform in Egypt* (I.B.Tauris, 2001).
2. Gathering or dissemination of statistics was subject to approval by the Central Agency for Public Mobilisation and Statistics (CAPMAS), created in 1964.
3. Terry Regier and Muhammad Ali Khalidi, 'The Arab Street: Tracking a Political Metaphor', *Middle East Journal*, 63/1 (Winter 2009), 11–29.
4. James Curran, 'Mediations of Democracy', in James Curran and Michael Gurevitch (eds), *Mass Media and Society* (Hodder Arnold, 2005), 145.
5. UNESCO International Programme for the Development of Communication, *Media Development Indicators: A Framework for Assessing Media Development*, CI-08/CONF.202/5 (Feb. 2008).
6. See Werner Rumphorst, *Model Public Service Broadcasting Law* (ITU/EBU/UNESCO, 1998), 1.
7. Steven Barnett, 'Broadcast Journalism and Impartiality in the Digital Age', in Gregory Ferrell Lowe and Jeanette Steemers (eds), *Regaining the Initiative for Public Service Media* (Nordicom, 2012), 204.
8. Relevant Penal Code articles include Nos. 174, 179, 184, 186, and 188–90. See Toby Mendel, *Political and Media Transitions in Egypt* (Internews, Aug. 2011), 8.
9. Soheir Hafez, quoted by Gihan Shahine and Hanan Sabra in 'Making Waves on Air', *Al-Ahram Weekly*, 640 (29 May–4 June 2003).
10. Curran, 'Mediations of Democracy', 139–41.
11. Quoted by *Daily News Egypt*, 'Alternative Media Grows, Restructures Industry', 12 Aug. 2011.
12. Author's interview, Cairo, 26 Jan. 2012.
13. Mai Shams El-Din, 'Activists, Journalists Launch Initiative for Public-Owned TV Channel', *Daily News Egypt*, 27 Oct. 2011.
14. Quoted by Maryam Raafat in 'Egypt Media Activists Plan "Public" TV', *Egyptian Gazette*, 28 Oct. 2011.

15 Quoted by Mai Shams El-Din, 'Activists, Journalists Launch Initiative'.
16 *Egypt Independent*, 27 Oct. 2011: http://www.egyptindependent.com/news/al-shaab-urid-tv-channel-postpones-initial-public-offering.
17 See James Curran's reflections on a hypothetical 'professional media sector', in 'Mediations of Democracy', 142.
18 Emad Mekay, 'People Funded TV Challenges Big Business', IPS News, 25 Aug. 2011.
19 Simba Russeau, 'Internet Radio Powers on After Arab Spring', IPS News, 14 Apr. 2012.
20 http://www.banat9bass.com/about_us.php.
21 Ayman Nour, quoted by *Daily News Egypt* in 'Al-Ghad Youth to Launch New Online Radio Station', 14 Sept. 2009.
22 http://ncmf.info/?p=117.
23 Ibid.
24 According to one of the protestors, quoted by Manal Ammar, 5 Oct. 2011: http://www.bikyamasr.com/44774/egypt-journalists-protest-plan-general-strike-against-scaf-over-press-oppression.
25 *Ahram Online*, 24 Oct. 2011: http://english.ahram.org.eg/News/24949.aspx.
26 Qatar Foundation press release, 21 Jan. 2012: http://www.ameinfo.com/287442.html.
27 Ami Ayalon, *The Press in the Arab Middle East* (Oxford University Press, 1995), 43.
28 Mohammed Kheir, 'Egypt's Press: Fuloul with a Twist of Brotherhood', *Al-Akhbar English*, 16 July 2011: http://english.al-akhbar.com/node/9862.
29 Central Auditing Organisation figure quoted by Omar Halawa, 'State-Owned Papers' Management Up for Grabs', 3 July 2012: http://www.egyptindependent.com/news/state-owned-papers-management-grabs-0.
30 Toby Mendel, *Political and Media Transitions in Egypt* (Internews, Aug. 2011), 8.
31 Translation by Nariman Youssef, published 2 Dec. 2012: http://www.egyptindependent.com/news/egypt-s-draft-constitution-translated.
32 Nathan Brown, 'Can the Colossus be Salvaged: Egypt's State-Owned Press in a Post-Revolutionary Environment?', *Carnegie Endowment Commentary*, 22 Aug. 2011.
33 Mona al-Naggar and Michael Slackman, 'Egypt's Leader Users Old Tricks to Defy New Demands', *New York Times*, 27 Jan. 2011.
34 As translated by Associated Press, 17 Sept. 2010.
35 Alexandra Sandels, 'The President's Man', 17 Nov. 2008: http://www.menassat.com/?q=en/news-articles/5152-presidents-man.
36 Matt Bradley and David Luhnow, 'Egyptians Take on Mini-Mubaraks', *Wall Street Journal*, 10 Mar. 2011.
37 Paul Adams, 'Al-Ahram's Own Revolution in Cairo', 18 Feb. 2011: http://www.bbc.co.uk/news/world-middle-east-12498705.
38 Ursula Lindsey, 'First Draft of History: Al-Ahram Finds a New Voice for Egypt', *Newsweek*, 13 Mar. 2011.
39 According to Mamdouh el-Waly, deputy editor for economic affairs at *Al-Ahram*, who was later elected to head the Journalists' Syndicate, quoted ibid.
40 Reem Leila, 'Same Old Story', *Al-Ahram Weekly*, 1106 (12–18 July 2012).
41 Sarah Carr, 'Bahais Flee Village After Attacks on their Homes', *Daily News Egypt*, 2 Apr. 2009.

42 Maurice Chammah, 'Debating Press Freedom in Egypt and Elsewhere', *Huffington Post*, 16 Nov. 2011: http://www.huffingtonpost.com/maurice-chammah/debating-press-freedom-in_b_1094977.html.
43 Shukrallah was removed from the English-language *Al-Ahram Weekly* in 2005 after establishing it as a relatively outspoken and dependable source of news and analysis. He became director of the Heikal Foundation for Arab Journalism and a founding editor of the privately owned newspaper *Al-Shorouk*.
44 AUC Press, 'Hani Shukrallah Explains his New Book's "Mea Culpa"', Oct. 2011: http://www.aucpress.com/t-eNewsletter-Shukrallah-October2011.aspx?template=template_enewsletter.
45 Arab Network for Human Rights Information press release, 7 June 2011.
46 Articles 55–6 of Ch. 1, sect. 3, in the translation used by Mendel, *Political and Media Transitions*, 7.
47 See the Executive Summary of the conference proceedings on the National Coalition for Media Freedom website: http://ncmf.info/?p=207.
48 http://www.guardian.co.uk/commentisfree/video/2011/jun/06/ibrahim-eissa-egypt-media.
49 Ibid.
50 Quoted by Nouran Al-Behairy, 'Journalists Believe Shura Council Criteria is [sic] "Islamisation" of the Press', *Daily News Egypt*, 8 July 2012.
51 Quoted by Omar Halawa, 'State-Owned Papers' Management Up for Grabs', 3 July 2012: http://www.egyptindependent.com/news/state-owned-papers-management-grabs-0.
52 Douglas Boyd, *Broadcasting in the Arab World* (Iowa State University Press, 1999), 16–18.
53 For details, see Toby Mendel, *Assessment of Media Development in Egypt* (UNESCO, June 2011), 25.
54 Indrajit Banerjee and Kalinga Seneviratne (eds), *Public Service Broadcasting: A Best Practices Sourcebook* (UNESCO, 2005), 15.
55 This is Menawy's figure in *Tahrir: The Last 18 Days of Mubarak* (Gilgamesh Publishing, 2012), 33. Reuters gave a higher figure of 46,000 in Feb. 2011.
56 Ibid., 101.
57 Quoted by Jack Shenker, 'Egypt's Media Undergo their own Revolution', *Guardian*, 21 Feb. 2011.
58 21 Feb. 2011: http://jackshenker.blogspot.co.uk/2011/02/state-media-revolution-and-violence-in.html.
59 Menawy, *Tahrir*; for example, p. 49.
60 http://www.bbc.co.uk/iplayer/episode/b01dbs3r/HARDtalk_Abdel_Latif_ElMenawy_Former_Head_of_Egyptian_state_news.
61 http://www.ifex.org/egypt/2005/09/06/election_coverage_favours_mubarak.
62 Quoted by Charles Levinson in 'Plus Ça Change: The Role of Media in Egypt's First Contested Presidential Elections', *Transnational Broadcasting Studies*, 15: http://www.tbsjournal.com/Archives/Fall05/Levinson.html.
63 Conversation with Jack Shenker, 'Egypt's Media Undergo their own Revolution', *Guardian*, 21 Feb. 2011.

64 *Egypt Independent*, 'Officials Accused of Squandering £E11bn', 15 Feb. 2011: http://www.egyptindependent.com/news/officials-accused-squandering-le11-bn.
65 Doaa El-Bey, 'New Faces, But ... ', *Al-Ahram Weekly*, 1042 (7–13 Apr. 2011).
66 Rana Khazbak, 'Seeds of Dissent in the State TV Fortress', *AlMasry AlYoum English*, 17 Nov. 2011: http://www.almasryalyoum.com/en/node/515364.
67 Quoted by Khazbak, ibid.
68 Menawy, *Tahrir*, gives the number as 3,000 on p. 107 and 3,500 on p. 34.
69 Ibid., 34 and 107.
70 Quoted by Rana Khazbak, 'State TV Staff Launches Protests to Demand Independence', *Egypt Independent*, 22 Jan. 2012: http://www.egyptindependent.com/node/614416.
71 http://www.ebu.ch/en/ebu_members/admission/index.php.
72 http://www.ebu.ch/en/union/news/2011/tcm_6-72864.php?display=EN.
73 See the text of the Charter at http://www.copeam.org/proj.aspx?ln=en&id=34&p=19.
74 Rasha Abdallah, *Media Diversity During Egypt's Parliamentary Elections (November-December 2011)* (Media Diversity Institute, Mar. 2012), 7–8.
75 Language used by two UK-based training consultants interviewed by the author, London, 18 June and 18 July 2011.
76 Author's interview, London, 18 June 2011.
77 http://www.tbsjournal.com/Archives/Spring05/ERTU.html.
78 Translation of an unedited contemporaneous note. The author's identity is protected.
79 BBC World Service Trust, *Annual Review 2006–07* (2007), 19.
80 The programme can be watched on YouTube, at the link posted by Randa El Tahawy, an audience member, in her *Egypt Today* article about the experience, at http://www.egypttoday.com/news/display/article/artId:583/Behind-the-Scenes-of-Questions-Time/secId:5/catId:22.
81 James Napoli et al., 'Privatization of the Egyptian Media', *Journal of South Asian and Middle Eastern Studies*, 18/4 (1995), 57. Hussein Amin, one of Napoli's co-authors, was at the time a member of the ERTU Board of Trustees.
82 *Enigma Magazine*, 'On Top with ONTV', 5 Sept. 2011.
83 Hijjawi, 'Role of Al-Jazeera (Arabic)', 70.
84 Quoted by Colleen Gillard, 26 Feb. 2012: http://www.bikyamasr.com/58693/how-the-arab-spring-has-transformed-journalism.
85 Hijjawi, 'Role of Al-Jazeera (Arabic)', 71.
86 Evidence gathered by Dan Murphy of the *Christian Science Monitor*, 8 Feb. 2011: http://www.csmonitor.com/World/Middle-East/2011/0208/Freed-Google-exec-Wael-Ghonim-reenergizes-Egyptian-protesters.
87 Abeer Allam, 'TV Channels Gripped by Vested Interests', *Financial Times*, 22 Dec. 2011.
88 Mohammed Al-Shafey, 'Asharq Al-Awsat Interview: Egypt's Information Minister Salah Abdul-Maqsoud', *Asharq al-Awsat*, 19 Sept. 2012: http://www.asharq-e.com/news.asp?section=5&id=31134.
89 Nathan Brown, 'Egypt's Ambiguous Transition', Carnegie Endowment for International Peace, 6 Sept. 2012: http://carnegieendowment.org/2012/09/06/egypts-ambiguous-transition/drsi#.

Chapter 4 Nuts and Bolts of a New Deal

1. http://www.ifj.org/en/pages/ifj-global-internet-and-new-media.
2. Aidan White, 'Ethical Journalism and Human Rights', in Council of Europe Commissioner for Human Rights (ed.), *Human Rights and a Changing Media Landscape* (Council of Europe, Dec. 2011), 70.
3. Yorck Von Korff, *Missing the Wave* (Deutsches Orient-Institut, 2003), 230–2; and Eberhard Kienle, *A Grand Delusion* (I.B.Tauris, 2001), 98–100.
4. *Al-Ahram* report quoted by Joel Beinin, 'The Rise of Egypt's Workers', Carnegie Middle East Centre, June 2012: http://carnegie-mec.org/publications/?fa=48689#.
5. Ibid.
6. Noha El-Hennawy, *Egypt Independent*, 20 July 2010: http://www.egyptindependent.com/news/school-teachers-form-egypts-2nd-independent-union.
7. Mostafa Abdelrazek, *Egypt Independent*, 2 Jan. 2011: http://www.egyptindependent.com/news/court-overturns-15-year-old-trade-syndicate-law.
8. See http://www.ejs.org.eg/Membership/MembershipConditions.aspx.
9. Mendel, *Political and Media Transitions*, 16.
10. Sarah Carr, 'Journalists Denied Syndicate Membership Go on Hunger Strike', *Daily News Egypt*, 21 Oct. 2008.
11. Yasmine Saleh, 'State-Backed Candidate Wins Press Syndicate Elections', *Daily News Egypt*, 18 Nov. 2007.
12. Mendel, *Assessment of Media Development*, 31.
13. Jano Charbel, *Egypt Independent*, 3 June 2011: http://www.egyptindependent.com/news/egypts-journalists-battle-organize-independently.
14. Quoted ibid.
15. *Daily News Egypt*, 'New Independent Press Syndicates Emerge', 6 May 2011. The International Journalists Network (www.ijnet.org) mentioned a similar Cairo-based project in a post in Dec. 2005.
16. Video of the interview was posted at http://www.mediainegypt.com/2011/12/egyptian-online-journalists-syndicate.html.
17. Video of the conference opening is available at http://www..youtube.com/watch?v=QUIHwHq_Bak.
18. Rana Khazbak, 'Seeds of Dissent in the State TV Fortress', 17 Nov. 2011, http://www.almasryalyoum.com/en/node/515364.
19. Author's interview, Cairo, 24 Apr. 2012.
20. Freedom and Justice Party website, 7 May 2012: http://fjponline.com/article.php?id=688.
21. Zeinab al-Gundy, 16 Nov. 2011: http://english.ahram.org.eg/NewsContent/1/64/26724/Egypt/Politics-/Egypt-Journalists-Syndicate-slams-military-trials-.aspx.
22. Sarah Mourad, 5 Apr. 2012: http://english.ahram.org.eg/NewsContent/1/64/38577/Egypt/Politics-/Egypts-journalists-syndicate-withdraws-from-consti.aspx.
23. Ahram Online, 1 December 2012: http://english.ahram.org.eg/NewsContent/1/64/59570/Egypt/Politics-/Press-syndicate-boss-rejects-discipline-over-role-.aspx.
24. Author's interview, Cairo, 24 Apr. 2012.
25. http://www.rjionline.org/MAS-Press-Councils-Indonesia.
26. UNESCO press release, 3 May 2012.

27 See pp. 3–4 of the *Guide*, which is posted as a pdf at http://ejn.globaleditorsnetwork. org/the-ethical-journalism-network-in-egypt.
28 Ibid., 7.
29 http://www.globalreporting.org/network/Organizational-Stakeholders/Pages/default.aspx.
30 Jennifer Bremer, 'Transparency of Egypt's Public-Private Joint Ventures', in OECD, *Towards New Arrangements for State Ownership in the Middle East and North Africa* (OECD, 2012), 137.
31 http://www.globaleditorsnetwork.org/ejn.
32 http://ejn.globaleditorsnetwork.org/the-ethical-journalism-network-in-egypt.
33 EOHR press release, Cairo, 12 May 2012.
34 *Der Spiegel International* online report, 7 July 2012.
35 Sarah El Deeb, Associated Press, 5 June 2012.
36 *Daily News Egypt*, 'NGO Trial Postponed Again', 5 July 2012.
37 State Information Service, 3 Aug. 2012: http://www.sis.gov.eg/En/Story.aspx?sid=63179.
38 http://pomed.org/wordpress/wp-content/uploads/2012/03/Egypt-NGO-Backgrounder-II.pdf, p. 4.
39 Exchange with ICFJ President Joyce Barnathan, published by ICFJ on 8 Mar. 2012.
40 Naomi Sakr, 'Public Service Media Initiatives in Arab Media Today', in Gregory Ferrell Lowe and Jeanette Steemers (eds), *Regaining the Initiative for Public Service Media* (Nordicom, 2012), 187–8.
41 Author's transcript of remarks on 27 June 2011, to a meeting sponsored by Internews at the Central European University, Budapest.
42 Ibid.
43 *Egypt Independent*, 20 June 2012: http://www.egyptindependent.com/news/egyptian-authorities-ban-use-carcinogens-textile-manufacturing.
44 http://i-m-s.dk/article/surge-investigative-journalism-post-mubarak-media, 18 Apr. 2011.
45 *Ahram Online*, 3 Oct. 2012: http://english.ahram.org.eg/NewsContent/1/64/54687/Egypt/Politics-/Draft-law-Foreign-NGOs-and-funding-still-require-p.aspx.
46 Jano Charbel, 15 Oct. 2012: http://www.egyptindependent.com/news/independent-unions-declare-new-alliance.
47 Reem Abou-El-Fadl, 'Beyond Conventional Transitional Justice: Egypt's 2011 Revolution and the Absence of Political Will', *International Journal of Transitional Justice*, 6/2 (2012), 318.

Bibliography

Secondary sources only; for primary sources see Notes section.

Abou-El-Fadl, Reem, 'Beyond conventional transitional justice: Egypt's 2011 revolution and the absence of political will', *International Journal of Transitional Justice*, 6/2 (2012), 318–30.
Ayalon, Ami, *The Press in the Arab Middle East* (Oxford University Press, 1995).
Banerjee, Indrajit and Seneviratne, Kalinga (eds), *Public Service Broadcasting: A Best Practices Sourcebook* (UNESCO, 2005).
Barnett, Steven, 'Broadcast Journalism and Impartiality in the Digital Age', in Gregory Ferrell Lowe and Jeanette Steemers (eds), *Regaining the Initiative for Public Service Media* (Nordicom, 2012), 201–18.
Bayat, Asef, *Life as Politics: How Ordinary People Change the Middle East* (AUC Press 2009).
Beinin, Joel, 'The Rise of Egypt's Workers', *Carnegie Middle East Centre* (June 2012), http://carnegie-mec.org/publications/?fa=48689#.
Black, Jeffrey, 'Egypt's Press: More Free, Still Fettered', *Arab Media and Society* (Jan. 2008), www.arabmediasociety.org/?article=572.
Boyd, Douglas, *Broadcasting in the Arab World* (Iowa State University Press, 1999).
Bremer, Jennifer, 'Transparency of Egypt's Public-Private Joint Ventures', in OECD, *Towards New Arrangements for State Ownership in the Middle East and North Africa* (OECD, 2012).
Chammah, Maurice, 'The Scene of the Crime: October 9th, Maspero, and Egyptian Journalism after The Revolution', *Arab Media and Society*, 15 (Spring 2012), http://www.arabmediasociety.com/?article=783.
Curran, James, 'Mediations of Democracy', in James Curran and Michael Gurevitch (eds), *Mass Media and Society* (Hodder Arnold, 2005).
Dabous, Sonia, 'Nasser and the Egyptian Press', in Charles Tripp (ed.), *Contemporary Egypt: Through Egyptian Eyes* (Routledge, 1993).
Deuze, Mark, 'The Professional Identity of Journalists in the Context of Convergence Culture', *Observatorio Journal*, 7 (2008), 103–17.
Diamond, Larry, 'Thinking about Hybrid Regimes', *Journal of Democracy*, 13/2 (Apr. 2002), 21–35.
Dubai School of Government, *Arab Social Media Report* (May 2011).
El Amrani, Issandr, 'Sightings of the Egyptian Deep State', *Middle East Report Online* (Jan. 2012), http://www.merip.org/mero/mero010112.

BIBLIOGRAPHY

Goldschmidt, Arthur, *A Biographical Dictionary of Modern Egypt* (Lynne Rienner Publishers, 2000).
Hallin, Daniel and Mancini, Paolo, *Comparing Media Systems* (Cambridge University Press, 2004).
Hammond, Andrew, *Popular Culture in the Arab World* (AUC Press, 2007).
Hijjawi, Aref, 'The Role of Al-Jazeera (Arabic) in the Arab Revolts of 2011', *Perspectives* (Heinrich Böll Stiftung), 2 (May 2011), 68–72.
Kassem, Maye, *Egyptian Politics: The Dynamics of Authoritarian Rule* (Lynne Rienner Publishers, 2004).
Kienle, Eberhard, *A Grand Delusion: Democracy and Economic Reform in Egypt* (I.B.Tauris, 2001).
Korany, Bahgat (ed.), *The Changing Middle East* (AUC Press, 2010).
Levinson, Charles, 'Plus Ça Change: The Role of Media in Egypt's First Contested Presidential Elections', *Transnational Broadcasting Studies*, 15, http://www.tbsjournal.com/Archives/Fall05/Levinson.html.
El-Mahdi, Rabab and Marfleet, Philip (eds) *Egypt: Moment of Change* (AUC Press, 2009).
El-Menawy, Abdel-Latif, *Tahrir: The Last 18 Days of Mubarak* (Gilgamesh Publishing, 2012).
Mendel, Toby, *Assessment of Media Development in Egypt* (UNESCO, June 2011).
Mendel, Toby, *Political and Media Transitions in Egypt* (Internews, Aug. 2011).
Miles, Hugh, *Al-Jazeera: How Arab TV News Challenged the World* (Abacus, 2005).
Napoli, James et al., 'Privatization of the Egyptian Media', *Journal of South Asian and Middle Eastern Studies*, 18/4 (1997), 39–57.
Osman, Ahmad, 'Rude Awakening: Dream Drops Top Talkers', *Transnational Broadcasting Studies*, 12 (Spring/Summer 2004), http://www.tbsjournal.com/Archives/Spring04/dream.htm.
Regier, Terry, and Ali Khalidi, Muhammad Ali, 'The Arab Street: Tracking a political metaphor', *Middle East Journal*, 63/1 (Winter 2009), 11–29.
Rumphorst, Werner, *Model Public Service Broadcasting Law* (ITU/EBU/UNESCO, 1998).
Saad, Reem, 'Shame, Reputation and Egypt's Lovers: A Controversy over the Nation's Image', *Visual Anthropology*, 10 (1998), 401–12.
Sakr, Naomi, 'Public Service Media Initiatives in Arab Media Today', in Gregory Ferrell Lowe and Jeanette Steemers (eds), *Regaining the Initiative for Public Service Media* (Nordicom, 2012), 183–98.
Sparks, Colin, 'Media and Transition in Latin America', *Westminster Papers in Communication and Culture*, 8/2 (June 2011), 154–77.
Springborg, Robert, 'Protest Against a Hybrid State: Words without Meaning?', in Nicholas Hopkins (ed.), 'Political and Social Protest in Egypt', *Cairo Papers in Social Science*, 29/2–3 (2009), 6–18.
UNDP, *Egypt Human Development Report 2010* (UNDP and Egypt National Institute of Planning, 2010).
UNESCO International Programme for the Development of Communication, *Media Development Indicators, A Framework for Assessing Media Development*, C1-08/CONF.202/5 (Feb. 2008).

Valeriani, Augusto, 'Pan-Arab Satellite Television and Arab National Information Systems: Journalists' Perspectives on a Complicated Relationship', *Middle East Journal of Culture and Communication,* 3/1 (2010), 26–42.

von Korff, Yorck, *Missing the Wave: Egyptian Journalists' Contribution to Democratization in the 1990s* (Deutsches Orient-Institut, 2003).

White, Aidan, 'Ethical Journalism and Human Rights', in Council of Europe Commissioner for Human Rights (ed.), *Human Rights and a Changing Media Landscape* (Council of Europe, 2011), 47–75.

Acknowledgements

Many more people deserve credit for any piece of research than can ever be adequately acknowledged. I am very grateful to David Levy at the Reuters Institute for commissioning this book and his great skill in advising on its content, and to David Gardner of the *Financial Times* for his helpful comments on the first draft. The fact that I was in a position to contemplate writing the report is thanks to Kristina Riegert at Stockholm University and Miyase Christensen at Karlstad University, who inspired me to focus on Egypt at a critical moment in 2011. The moment came soon after I co-organised a conference in Cairo in March 2011, under the title 'Rebuilding Egyptian Media for a Democratic Future'. For that I pay tribute to the drive and determination of the main organiser, Basyouni Hamada of Cairo University, and support received from colleagues at the Egyptian Ministry of Culture, University of Westminster Communication and Media Research Institute, and Open Society Institute. On a personal note, I would like to thank my husband, Ahmad Sakr, and Rasha Abdallah, Tarek Attia, Ali Belail, Alexandra Buccianti, David Dunkley-Gyimah, Nadine El-Sayed, Yosri Fouda, Naila Hamdy, Phil Harding, Hala Hashish, Adel Iskander, Lydia Khoury, Hafez al-Mirazi, John Owen, Milica Pesic, Abeer Saadi, Tamer Said, Jean Seaton, Biljana Tatomir, and Aidan White. We all owe an untold debt to the hundreds who died and thousands who suffered in and after the 25 January revolution to bring down dictatorship in Egypt.

[Handwritten margin notes:]
- On Bahrain, the "Pearl Roundabout phenomenon" of old-timers evoking a time before sectarian strife.

Provocative question: Do the likes of Al-Hurra, in pushing unevenly challenging programming, make it less likely that independent ventures will arise to do the same thing?

question: In Asian autocracies, how did journalism evolve?

RISJ/I.B.TAURIS PUBLICATIONS

CHALLENGES

Transformations in Egyptian Journalism
Naomi Sakr
ISBN: 978 1 78076 589 1

Climate Change in the Media: Reporting Risk and Uncertainty
James Painter
ISBN: 978 1 78076 588 4

Women in Journalism
Suzanne Franks
ISBN: 978 1 78076 585 3

EDITED VOLUMES

Media and Public Shaming: The Boundaries of Disclosure
Julian Petley (ed.)
ISBN: 978 1 78076 586 0 (HB); 978 1 78076 587 7 (PB)

Political Journalism in Transition: Western Europe in a Comparative Perspective
Raymond Kuhn and Rasmus Kleis Nielsen (eds)
ISBN: 978 1 78076 677 5 (HB); 978 1 78076 678 2 (PB)

Transparency in Politics and the Media: Accountability and Open Government
Nigel Bowles, David Levy and James T. Hamilton (eds)
ISBN: 978 1 78076 675 1 (HB); 978 1 78076 676 8 (PB)

The Ethics of Journalism: Individual, Institutional and Cultural Influence
Wendy Wyatt (ed.)
ISBN: 978 1 78076 673 7 (HB); 978 1 78076 674 4 (PB)